Nobody has more to say to men about manhood than Dave Dravecky. He's faced tests and trials, and passed them valiantly—so when he points to the possibilities for *any* of us, he's credible.

Jack W. Hayford
Senior Pastor, Church on the Way

This is a book you should read. Its concepts are ones that all of us need to make an everyday part of our lives.

John Trent, Ph.D.
President, Encouraging Words

In his loss, Dave discovered a depth of significance, security, value, and worth he had never known. Now he takes us back to the basics of God's Word, helping us go beyond who we think we are to become who God says we can be ... men of character and integrity.

Gary J. Oliver, Ph.D.
Author, *Real Men Have Feelings Too* and
How to Get It Right After You've Gotten It Wrong

Dave seeks to inspire men to find their God-given worth and identity. . . . Thankfully, most of us won't be called to walk the path that he has, but all of us can benefit from his journey.

Dr. John C. Maxwell
Founder, INJOY, Inc.

Dave takes on the fundamental issues of masculinity that every man worth his salt deals with. It took guts to write this book. It will take some guts to read it. But you will walk away a better man.

Steve Farrar
Men's Leadership Ministries

Books by Dave Dravecky

Do Not Lose Heart (with Jan Dravecky
and Steve Halliday)

Dave Dravecky (Today's Heroes) (with Tim Stafford)

Glimpses of Heaven (with Jan Dravecky
and Amanda Sorenson)

Stand by Me (with Jan Dravecky
and Amanda Sorenson)

The Worth of a Man (with C.W. Neal)

The
WORTH
of a
MAN

DAVE DRAVECKY
with C.W. Neal

ZONDERVAN™

GRAND RAPIDS, MICHIGAN 49530 USA

ZONDERVAN™

The Worth of a Man
Copyright © 1996 by David F. Dravecky

Requests for information should be addressed to:
Zondervan, *Grand Rapids, Michigan 49530*

Library of Congress Cataloging-in-Publication Data
Dravecky, Dave.
   The worth of a man / Dave Dravecky, with C.W. Neal.
      p.   cm.
   ISBN: 0-310-21942-6 (softcover)
   1. Men—Religious life. 2. Men—Conduct of life. 3. Identification (Religion)
4. Dravecky, Dave. I. Neal, C.W. (Connie W.), 1958– . II. Title.
   BV4528.2.D73   1996
   248.842—cd20   96-3747
      CIP

Published in association with Yates & Yates, LLP, Attorneys and Counselors, Suite 1000, Literary Agent, Orange, CA

Written by Dave Dravecky with C. W. Neal.

Printed in the United States of America

06 / ❖ DC / 10 9 8 7

Dedicated to my son, Jonathan.
May you always know
the true worth of a man.
"I love you, man!"

Contents

Acknowledgments

I find it hard to believe that Dave Dravecky, the baseball player, has (to some extent, anyway) become Dave Dravecky, the author. Who can help chuckling over this unexpected turn of events? But I am fully aware that there are a number of very special people behind the scenes who have made my transition to author possible. So let me take this opportunity to thank the people who helped make this project what it has become.

First, a special thanks to C. W. (Connie) Neal, whose vision, creativity, and tireless work helped lay the foundation for this book.

To the folks at Zondervan, my editors: Bruce Ryskamp, Scott Bolinder, John Sloan, and Verlyn Verbrugge. You are more than the publisher of my books; you are like family, and I am eternally grateful for all you have done for my own family.

To Jim Andrews: Even though you are now at home with our heavenly Father, you left behind a legacy of love to your kids that I hope I can leave behind to mine.

To Leslie, Daniel, Taylor, and Kevin Andrews: Knowing how difficult the past two years have been since Jim left this earth to be with Jesus, I am grateful for your allowing us to share your story. May God use it to encourage every man who reads this book.

To Chris Bingamin and Wayne McClure: Your lives have helped us to better understand God's love for all of us. Thanks for allowing me to share your stories. I trust they will be an encouragement to the men who will read this book.

To Bob Knepper: Thanks for reading this manuscript and giving encouragement as well as helpful insight into what men need as they seek to discover their true worth.

To Carla Muir: Thank you for your contribution to this book—the poem, "The Worth of a Man."

Thanks to those involved with the discussion groups, men and women who helped draw out my thoughts on the worth of a man: Jon Beebout, Bob and Robin Bertolucci, Larry Bertolucci, Loren Christopher, Carl Curtis, Gene Ebel, Frank Esquivel, Greg and Kathy Fairrington, Patrick Neal, Rick Roberts, Shawn and Jeanice Sullivan, Scott Vanderbeek, and Kelly Woods.

To Sealy and Susan Yates: You have been such an integral part of my life (our lives). Thank you for loving me, flaws and all.

To Steve Halliday, the special editor assigned to this project: Your commitment to excellence with this project has made it what it is. Thanks for helping me see my "true worth" before the One who has made me.

Last, but not least, I want to thank my wife, Jan, and my kids, Tiffany and Jonathan. Jan, your encouragement in the face of doubt and fear during this project allowed me to move forward and bring this book to completion. Thank you for loving me as you do. Because of that love, I have a greater sense of my true worth. And Tiffany and Jonathan, my love for you reminds me every day how much my heavenly Father loves me, despite all my flaws. You guys are the greatest!

Introduction:
Trading Cards and True Identity

When I was a kid and someone asked me, "What do you want to be when you grow up?" there was only one answer: "I want to be a major league baseball player." That wasn't what I wanted to *do* when I grew up; that's who I wanted to *be*. If only that dream could come true, I thought, my purpose in life would be fulfilled.

A Baseball Card

Today, a Dave Dravecky baseball card, encased in clear acrylic, sits on my desk. On one side there's a picture of me in my San Francisco Giants uniform. I'm on the mound, just about to blow the hitter away with a fastball. Seeing my card brings back memories of the intensity and passion with which I played the game. I'm reminded of how much I loved *be*ing a baseball player. The card makes me wish I could take the mound to pitch just once more. But I can't.

The back of the card lists my statistics. When I was playing the game, my stats were the most important part of the card to me. Clubs measure a player's worth by his stats. That's what determined whether or not you could continue playing in the major leagues. If you had a couple of good seasons, your stats showed it and you were rewarded substantially. If you had a couple of lousy seasons, the stats showed that too, and you were rewarded in the opposite way—they gave you the ax or traded you to another ball club.

Performance, measured by numbers, gave me a concrete way to measure my worth. I liked that because my stats were solid. I retired with a 3.13 lifetime earned run average and I won more than I lost, so I guess you could say I came away a winner.

When I was still a baseball player, I didn't realize how much I had tied my own personal worth to my career. Sometimes people would ask me where I got my sense of worth: from my career or my Christian faith? Huh? As if these issues are so easily defined! But back then I thought they were. I would always reply, "My worth and identity are found in Jesus Christ."

That was true, but it wasn't the whole truth. I didn't realize how much my identity and sense of worth came from my career ... until I lost it.

Back in 1989 when I was working hard toward making my comeback after cancer, I was pumping away on the exercise bike in the clubhouse, talking to my teammate and good friend Atlee Hammaker. We were carrying on a normal conversation, when all of a sudden Atlee asked me, "Do you think you'll miss the game if you can't come back and play?"

"No!" I immediately replied. "I won't miss the game. Baseball is not that important to me. It's more important that I'm a child of God, a father, and a husband. That's what's important to me. And the fact is, my career is going to come to an end sooner or later anyway."

But Atlee didn't believe me. "You mean to tell me, you won't miss baseball?" he demanded. "You've been playing this game your whole life—and you won't miss it?"

"That's exactly what I'm saying, Bud!" I declared. "I'm not going to miss it. There's more to my life than just being a baseball player!"

I insisted I wouldn't miss it—but I did. I missed it *bad*! As I sat home while the team was on the road, as I faced one operation after another, I recalled that discussion with Atlee more than once. He was right all along. I thought baseball hadn't meant that much to me, but losing my career was like losing part of myself. It's like the song says, "You don't know what you've got 'til it's gone."

I hadn't realized that baseball was more than just my career. It was the fulfillment of all my childhood dreams. It was my life. It gave me financial security and my sense of competence as a provider for my family. Baseball, I now admit, gave me my image, told me where I stood, identified whose team I was on and where I belonged in this world, and even measured my worth. My identity had been wrapped up in everything my baseball card represented, far more than I would previously have acknowledged.

There came a day, however, when my baseball card could no longer define my identity. When you wake up one morning and stare into a hospital mirror to see a man without a left arm and shoulder—and realize that guy in the mirror is you—you have to scramble to redefine your image. My left arm had been my strength; now nothing was there but empty space. I had invested all my efforts in baseball while denying other pursuits. If I didn't play baseball, what could I do to make a good living? If I wasn't a major league baseball player, who was I?

I'm afraid a Dave Dravecky baseball card today wouldn't trade for very much. Heck, it would have the pitching arm torn off. Trying to place a value on a current trading card of my life raises some interesting questions: What's the worth of a left-handed pitcher who doesn't have a left hand? Who am I now if I'm not Dave Dravecky, baseball player? What am I worth and to whom? Losing my pitching arm forced me to look deeper to find the worth of the man who had once been a major league baseball player.

In Search Of Worth

In this book, I want to challenge you to join me in this deeper search for our worth as men. You may never have been a major league ballplayer, but I'm pretty sure you've struggled (or will struggle) with the same kinds of questions about your worth that I have had to face about my own worth. If your life is your job and suddenly you lose it, what are you worth? If your identity is wrapped up in a wife and family and one day they are all gone, who are you? If your whole life is pointed toward achieving some goal and somehow it has eluded you, just what value do you have? Exactly what are you worth?

I'm not talking about the size of your bank account or the number of cars in your garage or the extent of your trophy collection. If these were all stripped away from you today—if all that was left was you—what would you be worth?

I did what few men have the privilege to do: I reached my boyhood dream. Yet while life as a baseball player was great, it did not give me the fulfillment I had expected. It did reward me tremendously, but the day still came when the baseball card with my picture on it became nothing more than a memento of past glories.

I'm glad I reached my dream, partially because I can tell those of you who never did so that fulfilling your dreams is *not* what proves your worth as a man. It took me awhile, but now I know I am worth as much today as I was the day I pitched a shutout during the National League playoffs. I have discovered that a man's true worth is found in who he is, not in what he does. And when a man makes that discovery, the world opens up like never before.

I'm Just A Lowly Penguin

In preparing to write this book, I spent four or five days with two groups of guys from Sacramento, California. What a tremendous time we had! We wanted to get a stronger grip on what it means to have worth as men. What is this worth? How does one get it? What difference does it make in the way one lives? We shared deeply from our hearts about our concerns, regrets, longings, hopes, and the things that puzzle us about ourselves.

I know it's impossible to recreate the dynamics of a group in the pages of a book, but I want to be able to get as close to the experience as possible. I want my readers to be able to benefit from the experience we enjoyed in Sacramento. How did we make such a great connection? The guys helped me put my finger on it.

"I know what it is," Rick volunteered. "Dave is a penguin."

"Say, *what?*" I thought he'd better clarify that one.

"You're a penguin. I've heard that whenever penguins are hungry and they need to go into the water to search for food, they find a hole in the ice and crowd around it. No one wants to be the first to go in because there might be a shark or some other predator waiting down there. So, they keep inching closer and closer together, nearer and nearer to the edge of the hole, until one penguin finally falls into the dark, icy water. The other penguins wait to see what happens. If the first bird in doesn't get eaten, the rest jump in with him and they all get enough to satisfy themselves.

"Dave, you're the first penguin in the water. Most men circle around the edge of the kinds of relationships that could satisfy them. They're all hungry, but afraid of what might happen to the one who's the first to be vulnerable, to admit weakness or fears. We've all seen enough guys eaten alive when they've ventured into those waters. But when somebody like you jumps in, hey!—the rest of us aren't afraid to jump in with you.

"You got us talking about issues we've all struggled with at one time or another. You admitted some of your flaws and conceded that you don't have it all figured out yet. You've admitted you're still hungry for a sense of your worth as a man. Once you did that, we could all jump into the conversation on a real level—just like the other penguins were convinced by the first penguin that it was okay to jump into the water."

So, according to Rick, I'm a lowly penguin. You know what? I think he's right! That's the role I sometimes play in this book. Not only will I share the principles that have helped me survive my rocky journey, but sometimes, when dealing with issues that still trouble me, I will simply be the first one to jump into the water by admitting my struggles.

I guess it's only fitting that I end up as a penguin. I actually began my college career as a Youngstown State Penguin. No kidding! That was our college mascot. I always thought it was a strange choice for a mascot, but I see now that it makes a lot of sense. It's really not so bad being a penguin. You might even get some exercise.

Join me for a swim?

Part One

My Journey to Find Worth

◆ ◆ ◆ ◆ ◆

Chapter One

Who Am I Now?

I was waiting to board a flight to Sacramento to work on this book. I held a ticket for a seat in coach, which didn't thrill me; and I was assigned a middle seat, which made it even worse. Who wants to sit in the middle? You never hear anyone say at an airline ticket counter, "Oh, by the way—do you have any middle seats left? I love being squashed between two people who would prefer my not being there at all. And it's so exciting not to know whether either of your armrests belongs to you or to the strangers who keep elbowing you back into your cramped little cubicle."

When we boarded the plane, I resigned myself to my position and informed the guy with the aisle seat that I would be sitting next to him. He let me in and I settled back, trying to get comfortable. Soon another man with a ticket for the window seat made his appearance and we shuffled around until everyone had taken his assigned place—one by the window, another by the aisle, and me squashed in the middle. I have to admit it; I wasn't looking forward to the three-hour flight under these conditions. But what can you do?

We started talking about the usual stuff: why we were heading to Sacramento and what we did. I told them I was going there to work on a book.

"Oh, you're an author?" asked the window man, whom we'll call Tom.

I don't know if he said it with a touch of skepticism or with genuine interest, but I replied, "Yeah, I find it hard to believe myself, but I am."

Then the aisle man, whom we'll call Fred, asked, "Well, what is it you're working on?" And Tom also wondered aloud, "What's your book about?"

I could tell they were genuinely interested, which surprised me a little. There I was, this one-armed guy who's pushing forty, obviously no sage. Yet they seemed genuinely intrigued by the prospect of hearing about the book. Who was I to deny their request? So I started describing the main idea.

"I used to be a professional ballplayer for the San Diego Padres and the San Francisco Giants," I said.

"What position?"

"Pitcher. I was a left-handed pitcher." I smiled, noting the irony that the left side of my upper body was now gone. "In 1988 doctors discovered a desmoid tumor in my upper arm. It turned out to be malignant, so they had to take out 50 percent of the deltoid muscle. The doctors told me that removing that much of the muscle would mean losing 95 percent of the use of my arm. They said I'd never pitch again, short of a miracle. But God did a miracle. Just a few weeks after the surgery, I could move my arm in ways the doctors said would be impossible. I went through ten months of physical therapy and on August 10, 1989, I made my comeback to pitch again in the major leagues. I pitched eight innings against the Cincinnati Reds and we even won the game."

Tom and Fred were nodding and making noises like they were starting to remember, so I kept going. "That comeback game was incredible. The fans, my family, my teammates— everybody seemed to go wild. They acted as if it were the greatest event in the history of the sport. Words can't describe how I felt standing on that mound as they flashed WELCOME BACK DAVE! on the big screen. I was inspired by what had happened as much as everybody else. They gave me something like nine standing ovations. It was incredible.

"Five days later, I found myself pitching against the Montreal Expos. We were ahead 3–0 in the bottom of the sixth inning and I was cruising. My arm was feeling a little strange, but it didn't hurt, so I kept going. Tim Raines came up to bat. He's a tough hitter and represented the tying run, so that's where my focus was. I ignored the tingling sensation in my arm. I threw a fastball . . . and . . . *crack!* It felt as if an ax had come crashing down on my pitching arm. I went flying off the mound, grabbing my left arm because it felt like it was ripping away from my body. I instinctively tried to keep it from flying off. When the bone in my arm snapped, it made a crack so loud my teammates heard it. I did a 360 and ended up writhing on the field . . ."

"That was on CNN, right?" Tom asked.

Fred said, "Yeah, I remember that story now. That was you? Were you on one of the morning shows?"

"Yeah, I was on all the morning shows. The media was all over us. Everybody wanted to know about the pitcher who made a comeback from what was supposed to be a career-ending injury, only to see his arm snap in mid-pitch on national television. The doctors said I could probably recover from the broken arm, even pitch again. Then two months later, when we won the National League pennant, I went out to the mound to celebrate with the team. I got caught in the crunch and broke my arm again, in a different place.

"At the end of the season I went through more tests. When the doctor again found cancer, my career came to an end. In January 1990 I underwent surgery for cancer a second time. Doctors also used some heavy-duty radiation treatments, in which radioactive elements were placed directly into my arm through catheters. The dosage was so strong that I had to be isolated for five days while I received the treatments. The radiation not only shrank the tumor, it also burned a hole in my arm that ulcerated, eventually growing to the size of a silver dollar. My son thought it was pretty cool that he could tap on the bone, but that was little consolation.

"In May 1990 I had to go for cosmetic surgery on the arm. They found more cancer and recommended more radiation. By September we thought we were out of the woods; then a serious staph infection appeared. Ten months later, in June 1991, it became clear what we had to do. The doctors suggested they remove my arm and shoulder to eliminate the risk of cancer spreading into my chest and possibly killing me."

"So, are you writing your story?"

"No, I wrote two books already: *Comeback* and *When You Can't Come Back*. This new one is about the worth of a man."

"What made you choose that topic?"

"When I lost my arm, I lost my career and my position; I really lost my sense of identity. All I had ever done was play baseball. Who was I, if not a pro baseball player? Battling cancer was hard enough, but working through issues related to my worth have been even tougher. It's been a long, hard journey. Today I can honestly say I'm better off for having been through it, but it hasn't been easy."

A Blessing in Disguise?

No, it hasn't been easy. I told the truth when I admitted that the task of identifying the real Dave Dravecky hasn't been a walk in the park. It's been painful, it's been hard, and many times I wasn't at all sure it was worth it.

But you know what? I'm glad now that I was forced to go through it. While the Dave Dravecky of a few years ago had a strong left arm that he used to pitch for the San Francisco Giants, he didn't have a very good idea of who he was. He made a lot of money and some pretty good headlines, but he had little idea of what he was truly worth as a man. And because he had only a dim idea of who he was and what he was worth as a man, there were many times he wasn't a very pleasant guy to be around. He wasn't very secure. He had a hard time relaxing. He knew precious little about *peace* and experienced even less of it.

Do I wish I still had my left arm? Sure I do. Yet I can honestly say that in these past few years I've gained far more than I lost. I am glad to be where I am now versus where I was before I got cancer. Three or four years ago, I couldn't have said that honestly; the good hadn't yet come out of the bad. Now I can even say that cancer has been a blessing in my life. What I learned through my battle with cancer is more valuable than what I understood about life before I was hit with adversity. I do not say this lightly or boastfully—I say this as one who has been humbled by pain and uncertainty—I would not be the man I am today if I had not been forced to fight cancer. I've still got a long way to go, but I have grown in ways I never dreamed possible because of the battle I had to fight.

I know many of the fans at Candlestick Park were saddened by what the cancer has done to my life. They didn't say it in so many words, but you could see in their eyes and hear in their voices that they thought it was a tragedy. I honestly don't feel that way.

There is a scene in the movie *Field of Dreams* where Ray Kinsella tracks down an old ballplayer named Moonlight Graham. Graham's career in the major league was so short it wasn't even a "flash in the pan." He played only a few minutes in one game. He never even got a chance to bat. That had been decades ago.

Graham was an old man now. He had become a doctor and had given his life to alleviate what sufferings he could in the small town where he lived. After talking about his experiences as a doctor, the two men get back to baseball. Kinsella can't get over how short Graham's career was: "For five minutes, you were that close to your dream. It would kill some men to be that close to their dream and not touch it. They would consider it a tragedy." Graham looks him in the eye and, with a wistful smile, says, "Son, if I'd only been a doctor for five minutes, now *that* would have been a tragedy."

Looking back over the past six years and seeing all I have learned from other people who have suffered; all I've experienced from other people's love; all God has shown me of his mercy and comfort; all the encouragement that my small measure of suffering has given to others; I think, *If I had continued on as a baseball player and missed that, now that would have been a tragedy!*

In a nutshell, that's why I've written this book. I want to try to help other men discover the same treasure I'm continuing to unearth myself: their true worth as men. But to do that, I think I should take you back a few years to a time that didn't look nearly so rosy.

A One-Armed Man

On June 18, 1991, Dave Dravecky became a one-armed man. Yet that's not when my identity crisis began. Before the amputation, my attention was consumed by all the medical treatments I was receiving—the surgeries, the radiation therapy, the medicine. I don't recall giving a second thought about what might come next for me. Even after my arm was amputated, I didn't allow myself to think a lot about who I was.

Right after I lost my arm, I stood in front of the mirror and said, "Look. This is the deck of cards that God has given me to play with. This is where I go from here. I'm an amputee. And so now I move forward with my life." I really thought, *What a great opportunity! I'm in the Sloan-Kettering Cancer Research Hospital, and now I can encourage others right here by sharing this experience I'm going through.*

At that time I thought I had to *do* more to *become* more like Jesus. I said to myself, *I'm going to go out there and do all of these wonderful things.* For the first five days after my amputation, I didn't focus on my own situation. Instead I was walking from room to room in the cancer ward, encouraging other people. That was the beginning of our current ministry to encourage cancer patients, amputees, and their families. On that day Jan and I started to travel around the sixteenth floor—my floor—and to present the patients with gifts. We received so many flowers that we decided to give them out to people who didn't have any. We had received food baskets, too, so we distributed those as well. We became friends with a lot of people that way.

During the six days at the hospital following my surgery, I was energized. I didn't think about the loss of my arm. I was cruisin'. I thought, *Hey, this isn't so tough after all.*

Today I think that, deep down inside of me, there were issues that I simply didn't want to face. I didn't consciously go out and start interacting with people so I could forget about the loss of my arm, but I think subconsciously that was a major motivation for what I did. I wanted to be involved in other people's lives so I wouldn't have to think about my own struggles.

In fact, I saw my activity as a unique opportunity. It was yet another way that I could please God through a good performance. I mean, why wouldn't he be pleased that a professional baseball player—a pitcher, no less—would go out and encourage people right after his left arm had been cut off? How could God not be impressed with a man who, just a scant twenty-four hours after he lost his arm, was out there serving others? I thought it was a pretty neat thing to do, so that's what I did.

When I was released from the hospital to return home, the doctor instructed me to spend July and August relaxing and doing nothing. "Allow yourself to be pampered," he ordered, "and then from there we think you can get back out on the speaking circuit, if that's what you decide to do." Prior to the amputation, I had accepted several speaking engagements between various therapies and treatments.

I was a good boy. I followed doctor's orders, went home, kicked back, and relaxed. I didn't do much for two whole months. I had to deal a little with phantom pain and a few other "amputee" issues, but for the most part it was a pretty smooth transition. During those two months I never thought much about the big question: Who am I now? Periodically I would stand in front of the mirror and think, *Wow, there's really a lot gone.* But the reality of what I was missing never sank in.

As my recuperation period came to a close, however, I had to decide what to *do*. I couldn't sit around the house all day; neither Jan nor I would go for that. So what would I do? I wouldn't be making any more comebacks to professional baseball, at least not as a pitcher. But if I wasn't Dave Dravecky, pitcher for the San Francisco Giants, who was I?

Why Am I Here?

Why am I here? What am I supposed to do? I racked my brain with those questions while facing what to do next. I thought about coaching college ball. I considered working with baseball chapel. I debated working for Focus on the Family. I thought about a lot of things, each a different version of: What am I supposed to do with my life *now*?

I never stopped to ask myself such questions before the amputation. I simply took the talent I had and used it to carve out a satisfying career. It was only when the career was over that I had to ask the tough questions about the purpose of my life. And I didn't like it—not one bit.

I'm a guy who likes to *do* things. I wanted to jump right into doing something else, but I discovered there is a process one has to go through first. Zig Ziglar, whom I respect highly, said, "You've got to *be* before you can *do*, and you've got to *do* before you can *have*." That was a big part of my problem. The only thing I knew how to *be* was a baseball player. How could I be something else? Yet I had to be something else; my empty left sleeve constantly reminded me of the fact.

So, Dravecky: Who are you? What are you going to do now? What's the plan, Bud?

And I had no idea. It was my turn at bat, I was behind 0 and 2, and I had no clue how to hit the next pitch. I didn't even know what kind of pitch it might be.

Talk about an identity crisis!

When a man is forced to evaluate who he is, he faces a struggle most of us are unprepared for. I know I was. We look for fulfillment in reaching our boyhood dreams, in fame and fortune. If we never reach our dreams—or reach them and lose them, or find ourselves unsatisfied once we fulfill them—we get confused. We may then define ourselves by our *dis*abilities or our *lack*. I know how that feels. You tell yourself you're nothing anymore and that you don't have much to offer. When I left baseball, I didn't feel competent to do anything else. But I had to do *something*. What would it be?

I decided to return to an activity I did know a bit about (not much, but a little; at least it was more than nothing). I returned to the speaker's circuit and started making appearances in as many places as often as I could. Believe me, it got crazy. I remember doing a trip to California. I spoke eight times in four cities in five days. At the end of that trip, to no one's astonishment but my own, I was exhausted.

I came home, flopped on the bed, looked up at Jan, and moaned, "You know, this is ridiculous. I don't feel like a whole man. I don't know why I'm doing this. I know I'm not enjoying it. I feel like a hypocrite." Right there in our room, without the benefit of balloons, hats, or noisemakers (other than me), I was holding a pity party. "Here I am, giving to everybody else," I muttered, "and no one is giving back to me." It wasn't true, of course, but that's what it felt like to me.

As I lay on our bed, complaining and staring up at an unresponsive ceiling, I was convinced I had hit rock bottom. I was being forced to do something I had so diligently avoided. It was time to look in the mirror and face reality. For several months after the amputation, I wouldn't face the truth. I didn't allow myself to think about it. I didn't ponder the loss of my arm or what it would mean in relation to what I would do with my life and who I was—all those questions that now came bubbling up into the open like hot, acidic gas from a crack in an active volcano.

But that wasn't the worst of it. Prior to all my struggles with cancer, I could sit back and confidently say, "To live is Christ, and to die is gain." But when I was diagnosed with cancer, suddenly I found I couldn't so glibly say that anymore. I didn't *want* to die—so had I really identified with Christ? Was I truly connecting with this person in whom I had placed my faith and trust? Or was my faith just another example of a person who talks about having a relationship with God, not a religion, but who continues to act as if it is a religion, not a relationship? Part of all religion is lip service, saying the right things. Is that all I had been doing?

These hard questions did not go away when I went back out on the lecture circuit. In fact, they intensified. While the threat of imminent death had been removed along with my left arm and shoulder, my inner struggle grew. Soon I reached the point of saying, "Am I really a Christian? I mean, if I can't identify with Christ here in my painful ordeal, do I really know him?"

Please don't misunderstand; there never came a time when I gave up on the faith. It was just that, at this time, I was confused about where I stood spiritually. All along I had insisted to everyone that my faith had been my anchor—and now it felt as if my ship were drifting and making me very, very seasick.

That was my real struggle. That was the crux of my identity crisis. At that point, quite frankly, it didn't make any difference to me what I was "worth"; I just wanted to have a clear sense of who Dave Dravecky was, post-baseball. Despite what I had so confidently declared to Atlee Hammaker in the clubhouse, I now found that my identity really had been wrapped up in my left arm. It had brought me joy. It had brought me money. It had brought me status, nice homes, and nice cars. I was unprepared for the discovery that so much of my identity was wrapped up in that arm and what it was capable of doing.

Or rather, what it *had been* capable of doing. With a few flicks of a surgeon's scalpel, it was gone forever. All of a sudden, I found myself in no-man's-land. I didn't know who I was. I felt guilty because all along I'd been telling everyone that my identity was not in playing professional baseball, but in being a Christian—and now I was wondering whether I was a Christian at all. The crunch was on, and I didn't know if, in fact, Dave Dravecky was even saved.

If that won't send a guy into depression, I don't know what will.

Chapter Two

Exhausted and Depressed

I t took an act of God to convince me that I was depressed.

I never grieved the loss of my arm. Instead, I went on automatic pilot, trying to survive the medical ordeal, while stuffing my feelings under the surface.

While I had cancer, we attended a church that taught it was impossible for a Christian to be depressed if he or she were truly walking with the Lord. I bought into that teaching and denied all my symptoms (as well as Jan's) of depression. In that setting, admitting that I was depressed and seeking professional help would have been like confessing sin. I really believed that if I kept a positive attitude and kept trying to help others, I could and should get around my own grief without going through it.

I was wrong.

After the amputation, there actually was a sense of relief in that the immediate threat of cancer was removed. So I genuinely praised God for my life and the opportunities he gave me, and I just kept going full speed ahead. Meanwhile, Jan had been falling apart emotionally even before my arm was amputated. She begged me to let her get help. She was crying all the time and basically became bedridden. Yet I couldn't admit that she was depressed, much less that I was.

As an athlete, I had learned how to push past the pain. If I stopped pushing myself whenever I felt physical pain, I never would have made it to the big leagues. So naturally I applied the same jock mentality to emotional pain—and it didn't work.

Living A Double Life

Do you know what it's like to live a double life? I do. I could put on a good show. In terms of performance, I was at the top of my game, sharing my testimony and playing the triumphant role I had taken on after my comeback.

But when I came home, I acted like a jerk.

Today I realize that I was depressed, though at the time I didn't even know the signs. I put out a lot of energy on the road and then let down when I came home. I would "veg out" by hiding at home when I was supposed to be at the office. I didn't feel like going in because it was too hard to pick up the phone and call people who were hurting. I kept procrastinating and doing a lot of things to avoid having to deal with other peoples' pain and suffering. To say that I was hard to get along with would be a diplomatic way of describing the situation.

While I was going through this phase, Bob, a friend of mine, called me a couch potato. He only said aloud what a lot of people were thinking. No one saw me doing a whole lot. So I decided to show Bob what it was like on the road. Remember the trip to California where I scheduled myself to speak eight times in five days in four cities? I took Bob with me on that trip to prove that my work was strenuous.

That week I spoke to group after group, giving my testimony of how God gave me the miraculous comeback, how he used my fall from the mound to give me a platform for sharing my faith, and how I accepted the loss of my arm as part of God's overall plan for good in my life. It all sounded so wonderful.

But beneath the words, the man beneath the image of the victorious Christian was suffering and afraid to let anybody know. While I spoke to thousands on that trip, I wanted nothing more than to be alone. I didn't even talk to Bob; I didn't want him to see how I was feeling inside. So I just kept quiet.

After I returned home, I hit bottom. I lay on the bed and said to Jan, "Forget it! I don't want to talk about Jesus anymore." I was depressed about my appearance; I saw myself as disfigured. I asked Jan, "How could you love me? I'm not even a whole man anymore!"

Jan reassured me of her love, but I had a hard time receiving it. She even said to me, "I know you can't cry, so I'll cry for you." My changed appearance wasn't the only thing I was struggling with, however; deeper things inside were bubbling to the surface.

For one thing, I felt like a hypocrite. I would go on stage to speak to a men's group or a church and act like everything was great, but when I came home I was miserable. I scorched my family with ugly outbursts of anger. At that time, I didn't like myself a whole lot. I was hurting, and I got to the point where I was tired of faking it. I was tired of going out and acting one way, then coming home and acting another. How could a real Christian act as I was acting? Finally I decided it had to be either one or the other; I could not go on playing the game.

At this low point in my life, I was scheduled to speak to the "Gathering of Men" (an event similar to Promise Keepers), held in West Palm Beach, Florida. I was sitting in my room the day of the event and was in no mood to go out and speak. I was exhausted from struggling with the conflict raging inside of me. I had no desire to talk to anyone, to encourage anyone, to tell anyone about Jesus. I thought, *Enough! I've had it.*

Jan didn't accompany me on the trip, but she knew I was down and tried to encourage me. She even had a friend call to give me a pep talk. He prayed for me over the phone, but nothing was working. My agent, Sealy Yates, called and said some really helpful things. He prayed with me, too—and yet when I got off the phone, I thought, *It doesn't matter. I still don't want to do it. I'm just not in the mood to be here right now. I'm tired of putting on a good show.*

Jan called again and I told her, "You know, I'm just sick of this. I don't have any desire to go out and tell these men about Jesus and a relationship with him. I don't even know what my relationship with him is anymore. I'm exhausted. I'm just tired of this whole thing. I don't want to do this anymore. I want to quit. I think I'm depressed—and if I'm not, well, what am I doing here?"

Jan didn't argue with me. She just listened and tried to comfort me. She promised she would pray for me and then got off the phone. She called back a few minutes later. I'll never forget what she said because it made me see that I couldn't go on being a double-minded man. She said, "Dave, you've got two choices. You can go out there and fake it, if that's what you want to do. Be an encourager, tell them about Jesus, and pretend like you're doing great. Or you can go out there and tell them how you really feel."

"Oh sure, I'll just tell them I'm feeling lousy," I replied, the sarcasm in my voice unmistakable. "I'll say, 'I don't want to be here. I don't want to talk to you and I don't want to tell you about Jesus!' That should come off real good!"

"You have to choose," Jan repeated. "Go out there and fake it, or go out there and tell them the truth and let God use you in whatever way he can after you're honest." Then she left me to decide.

Moments later, in front of five hundred men who were expecting me to pump them up with some inspirational talk, I said, "You know what? This is something totally different than what I had planned to share with you tonight. The fact is, I don't feel like being here. I have no desire to share my story with you. I have no desire to tell you about Jesus. I don't have the strength even to be here. God will be the judge of whatever comes out of my mouth tonight. I'm depressed and I don't know what's going to happen. But I have to be honest with how I feel, because I'm totally sick of playing games. That's it."

I didn't know what to expect, but the men were extremely receptive. They accepted me at a time of weakness and affirmed me. A number of men came up afterwards and said, "I'm so grateful that you shared that. Do you know how many times I've felt like chucking it all? Do you know how many times I've felt like I can't say I'm depressed? Now, I've got a reason to tell someone the truth about what I'm going through. Thank you so much."

Frankly, I think the response was so positive because I was vulnerable. That was a big surprise to me. I don't think I ever would have risked what I did had I not come to the point of exhaustion. When I realized, *Hey, these guys really accept me for who I am!* I could hardly believe it. It felt good. I felt closer to those men than I had to any previous group.

That night was a turning point in my life and in my speaking career. I still had a long way to go, but that night I finally realized the value of being flat-out honest instead of trying to fake it. That is when I decided to do my best to be open about what was going on inside.

When I thought I had to put on a good show, I was wearing out and I felt used by people. I felt sucked out until there was nothing left to suck out anymore. When I let my real self show and found acceptance instead of rejection, I began to see that I didn't have to pretend. While I was spilling out the truth about how drained I felt, God started filling me up with the acceptance of these men. I went out of there charged up instead of wiped out.

Being honest about how I felt freed me from thinking I had to be a certain way for one group of people and then go back to my family and be the real me. The double standard in my life had been draining my strength and alienating me from those closest to me. After that night, I decided it was okay to be real, even if the show wasn't always so good.

Another Step Taken

Even though the Gathering of Men was a beginning for me, it was only that—a beginning. I was still afraid to talk in depth about what I was feeling.

My struggle went all the way back to Atlee Hammaker and his question about whether I would miss the game of baseball. Until I was finally able to admit that I was depressed, I didn't realize that I had been denying the pain inside of me. I denied that I had lost something, that I had lost my identity.

To refuse to admit that I really did miss and enjoy the game was foolish. It had been such a major part of my life. It was wonderful being a baseball player; baseball brought me a lot of joy. And in a real sense, the game did help to define my identity at that stage of my life, to explain my place in the world and who I was.

Trying to re-identify myself was extremely difficult. When all you've done is play baseball, and then at the prime of your career the rug is pulled out from under you, there's a great deal of adjusting that has to take place. I have described part of that struggle in *When You Can't Come Back*.

I now believe that one of the chief things that led to the depression is that I made a common error: I had confused my *identity* with my *worth*. I was thinking my worth was wrapped up in my identity, but that wasn't true. During one season of life, my place in this world really could be identified by my connection to professional baseball; yet that never meant that my worth as a man was tied to my vocation. I was worth just exactly as much after the amputation as I was when I was pitching—but when you equate your current *identity* with your unchanging *worth*, you're in for big trouble. And that is exactly what I had done. So it is no wonder I ended up depressed.

Anatomy of a Depression

It might be helpful at this point to look more closely at the reasons behind my depression and how they relate to the issue of worth. While my particular circumstances won't match that of many others, I think the root causes of such depression are pretty common.

As already mentioned, immediately after the amputation I started visiting people on my floor, trying to encourage them and help them however I could. I thought this kind of activity would please God. I was sincere, but I didn't realize two things:

1. Once again I was *performing* to please God;
2. I was *hiding from the reality of pain inside* over the loss of my arm and career.

In my life as a baseball player I constantly had to please and entertain others. Especially as a *Christian* baseball player, I was there to live out my life to please God; I performed to please him. Now in my life after baseball, I went right back into that same mode.

I believe there is a time in most of our spiritual journeys when we confuse service to God with our walk with him. This is where Jan and I were at this point; we automatically slipped into that mode in our relationship with God. And it did fill a void, at least for awhile. We felt as if we were pleasing God and doing something for those who needed help—and besides, it gave us strokes.

So I continued to perform, this time for God. I served the Lord in the midst of our struggles. But in the process, I was covering up the pain inside—something I had been doing since childhood.

I was not used to dealing with issues of pain. My habit was to get on with life and not think about it. I would try to concentrate on the positive and ignore what was going on inside. After years of doing that, you get locked into a pattern and it doesn't make any difference whether you're a Christian or not. Perhaps it should, but it doesn't seem to. Just because Jesus lived in my heart, I didn't all of a sudden act differently from the way I'd been living for thirty plus years. My actions continued to be governed by an old attitude: "I'm going to be positive about this. I'm going to try to forget it. If I don't think about it, it'll go away." That's not what the Scripture teaches, but at that point in time, I didn't especially care what the Scriptures said. What I was doing seemed to be working, and that was enough.

I suppose I was like Scarlett O'Hara—"Tomorrow is another day." I just wouldn't worry about it right now; I would put it out of my mind. What better way to do that than to get busy in the name of Christianity? So I served others out of a sincere, but ignorant, heart.

Tired, Tired, Tired

My way of dealing with pain soon pushed me into unhealthy habits that inevitably lead to depression. And what finally triggered the depression? I can tell you in one word: exhaustion.

Four months after the amputation, three things came to the forefront:

1. I was physically exhausted and burned out.
2. I struggled with understanding how to communicate my pain, fear, and doubt.
3. I came face-to-face with the reality of my own weakness, which at first was hard to admit.

As an athlete, I took pride in my physical endurance. I wanted to think, *I can go out there and pitch for nine innings, get a complete game.* I took pride in pointing to several complete games on my stats. And I carried that attitude into the way I was going to handle the amputation. "I'm going to endure this process," I told myself. "I'm going to take charge and I'm going to get through it. Whatever it takes or however much I have to do, I can handle it. There's no question about it; I can handle it. If I can handle being a major league baseball player, I can handle just about anything." But it wasn't true.

By pushing as hard as I did, I ended up burning out. I reached the point where I just couldn't go on anymore. I couldn't handle any more speaking. Of course, nobody in their right mind makes a commitment to speak eight times in five days in four cities. A sane person just doesn't make that kind of promise—but I made it because I thought I was superhuman. I had been given a message from God for people who were suffering, and I was going to deliver it.

As a result, I ended up exhausted. To this day, I can't clearly remember those months; it's a blur, as though I were living in a fog. One thing I do know is that I didn't have a whole lot of energy. I moped a lot.

The hectic schedule wasn't the only thing that exhausted me, however. Trying to do things with my remaining hand—the nondominant one at that—made me very tired. I was constantly fumbling around with my clumsy right hand. I had always worked well with my hands, and now I was fumbling all over the place. That exhausted me.

And pain itself is exhausting. Having to mentally deal with pain, day in and day out, sapped my energy. The phantom pain could be unbelievable. In my mind, my left hand would cramp up. Just to release the cramp I would mentally have to pry loose my missing fingers. Sometimes the ends of my fingers felt like they were burning.

This kind of phantom pain still occasionally hits me. Even nowadays I can feel my missing arm as much as I feel my right— probably more so, unless I flex. It's all there. Even as I'm working on this chapter, my mind tells me that my missing left hand is cramped. Since those early days I've learned how to deal with it; I just leave it alone. Eventually there's a little buzz, something like an electrical charge. All of a sudden—zzzzt!—it releases. But in the beginning, it was extremely taxing. It was only by the grace of God that I was allowed to sleep.

Jan believes that another cause of my exhaustion came in the form of demands placed on me by others. I'll let her explain:

> Beyond the physical causes of exhaustion, what was really hard were the expectations placed on Dave, not only by others outside, but even by me. He had this attitude of laughing all the time. He just had this great patient attitude. He was easy to take care of at that point. He wasn't feeling sorry for himself, he wasn't crying. You would forget what he was going through. You would forget that he was going through the phantom pain. You would forget how exhausting it is to be in constant pain. You'd forget that he's having to adjust to life.
>
> Because it seemed he was doing so well, we started to assume that he should *do* everything well. We thought he should be doing this and that; he just had so many expectations placed on him during that time.

37

I believe Dave and I still bought into the lie that where there's opportunity, we should "go for it." We thought if God had created the opportunity, we had to take it. We hadn't yet developed the personal side to our relationship with the Lord enough to know when to say yes and when to say no. We hadn't yet learned how to really listen for his voice.

Beyond the exhaustion, one of the most difficult things for me was having to admit certain things about myself. I had to admit I was afraid, and no athlete ever wants to admit he is afraid. When you admit you're afraid, you lose control over the situation—and you can't *ever* lose control. You have to be mentally on top of it. You have to be mentally tough.

Fear is not in the vocabulary of being mentally tough. Neither is doubt. If you go out on the mound and you doubt whether you can get somebody out, you've already lost half the battle. On the other hand, if you're mentally tough, you know you can get the guy out, so half the battle's already won.

I had been programmed for so many years not to admit fear, not to have doubts, but rather to be strong and confident, to be a conqueror. When these emotions of fear and doubt hit, it was like a tidal wave engulfing me. It was one thing to admit pain, but this was something else.

What especially bothered me was the fear of death. Even as a Christian, the fear of dying consumed my thoughts. I did not want to die. It wasn't so much the fear of death itself, because deep down there was a peace; I certainly didn't feel peace, but I knew it was there. Still, I didn't know what dying involved and how I was going to die. All I knew was that I wanted to be around. I loved my wife and kids and I didn't want to leave them. The fear of losing them consumed me.

The Role of Good Counseling

Not until the Gathering of Men did I open up about what I was feeling. Even then I still didn't deal with the internal issues that were churning inside—the fears and the doubts. That didn't come until I became willing to admit I was depressed. And that didn't take place until I was actually in counseling with Jan.

I only went with Jan to counseling in the first place to appease her. I finally grudgingly admitted that she needed help. So I said, "I love you, and because I love you, I will be there for you." It was almost out of obligation to my marriage that I committed to be there for her.

But about three weeks into the counseling, I realized I was just as depressed as Jan was. Suddenly I was the one on the couch! So a scant four months after the amputation, Jan and I were both in a counselor's office, depressed. But what a wonderful place to make such a discovery! Bit by bit I began to understand the value of opening up and talking about my weaknesses. There I was, for the first time opening up my heart—and what came out was, "I'm scared. I'm afraid. I don't want to die. I'm not sure about my faith. I'm weak. Look at me."

You know, there's great freedom in admitting that truth. The truth of God's Word sets you free, but so does the truth about yourself. There's wonderful freedom in knowing you don't have to be anything but what you truly are.

When I finally began to confess with my mouth what I truly was, I found both freedom and cleansing. I couldn't help it if the world wanted a hero; I am not a hero. I am not anything but Dave Dravecky. I am a sinner saved by grace, and there's great freedom in admitting that. As I started to understand and admit my weaknesses, I felt a great weight being lifted from me. It had been there far too long.

Chapter Three

A Hard, but Necessary, Admission

I don't like weakness. I don't suppose most men do. We don't want to talk about what is really going on inside of us—the self-doubts, regrets, or fears. Yet no matter how much we dislike weakness, the word accurately describes who we are in one area or another. To deny the fact simply makes life difficult. I know; I made life difficult for my whole family when I refused to admit my own weakness.

Jan is one of the strongest people I know. Before I finally agreed to go to counseling, I thought she could handle anything. But life had not treated her kindly. Besides all of my ordeals, both her parents had recently died, she was trying to respond to all the mail and media requests we were getting, she was taking care of me and putting up with my moods, and on top of it all she was trying to care for the kids. Soon she collapsed under the weight of it all. That's when the panic attacks began.

Helpful husband that I was, I tried to tease her out of her attacks by mimicking one of them. I thought she should be able to rise above our problems. When I realized she couldn't, I got mad. I'm ashamed to admit it, but I became furious with her. The more adamant she was about her need for professional help, the angrier I got. For months I stubbornly refused to let her see a counselor. I didn't like weakness, and I suppose I felt my wife's problems were a reflection on my own inability to help her.

Jan didn't want to defy me, so she relied on whatever relief she could find in self-help books at the Christian bookstore. At that time the Lord led us to a church where one of the associate pastors had gone through an inpatient treatment program for depression. His wife had worked for the Minirth-Meier Clinics. By talking to them, Jan realized help was available. But when she again tried to talk me into letting her get treatment, do you know what I did? I blew up! I threw the phone across the room, busted it to pieces, and told her to go ahead and call. She made the only call she could, calling out to God and asking him to get through to me, since she couldn't.

A few weeks later we were scheduled to appear on the Focus on the Family radio broadcast for the third time. We met with Dr. Jim Dobson before the broadcast, and he asked Jan how she was doing. She admitted she was having a hard time emotionally. She didn't tell him how stubborn I had been, but she did ask what he thought of getting professional help for depression. He thought it was a healthy approach to our situation. Then Dr. Dobson asked me why the thought of Jan getting professional help upset me. He asked whether I thought it was my job to fix her. The thought had never occurred to me, but today I think he was right on target.

I did think I was supposed to fix her problem, but I didn't know how. I *was* sure, however, that I didn't want to let anybody else try to fix it. That would mean I was unable to do it myself, and that would imply weakness. I think that's why I got so angry. The idea that I couldn't fix Jan's problem challenged my idea of who I was as her husband. I always wanted to take care of my wife, and I thought that if I admitted she needed counseling, then I had failed in my role as husband.

After the broadcast, Dr. Dobson urged me to allow Jan to get whatever help she needed from competent Christian therapists. By the time we got home, I was willing to let her call, but God was ahead of me. The very next day, my agent, Sealy Yates, gave Jan a book by Henry Cloud. It just so happened (ha!) that she already had been reading it. Sealy told us that Dr. Cloud was one of his clients, and he arranged for Jan and me to meet with Dr. Cloud's partner, Dr. John Townsend.

When we sat down with John, he said point blank, "Dave, your wife is sick and she needs help—and you are not the one to help her. Furthermore, you're depressed, too. You're just as messed up as your wife is. Both of you are off the chart in terms of the amount of stress you've been under. It's a wonder you're both still alive and still married."

That was an answer to prayer for Jan and a slap upside the head for me. It knocked some sense into me and I agreed to go to counseling with her. Yet the decision to go for counseling was very difficult. It meant I had to admit I needed help, and that would mean I was weak. So I had to struggle with that issue first: *How much is it worth to get my wife help? Is it worth exposing a weakness in my life and saying I need someone to fix me, when all along I've been able to fix just about everything that has come across my path?*

Admit Weakness, Lose Control

I think most men are afraid of showing their weakness because it causes them to lose control. When I was in baseball, I talked very little about what was going on in my heart with the guys in the clubhouse. To open up like that was a sign of weakness, and to show weakness means to lose control. Ballplayers don't dare make themselves vulnerable. They don't expose their weakness; instead they hide it, talk about surface issues, and don't let other people in.

In baseball, I knew if I ever let down my guard for one minute, I'd be eaten for breakfast by the other guys. I knew the rules without anybody having to tell me. One of the primary rules was: Don't ever say that you are scared. If you do, you're history. They're gonna walk all over you.

Yet keeping fear to myself almost cost me my big league career before it ever got started. When the Padres first called me up, I was overwhelmed by a series of big events. Two days before I got the call—the call I had been waiting for my whole life—I became a father. Now I thought, *Well, I'm a big leaguer; I have to be tough.* But fear got to me. For the first ten days, everybody who came to the plate looked like Babe Ruth, and I couldn't get anybody out. Inside I was thinking, *What the heck is going on here? Maybe I'm not cut out to be a big league ballplayer.* The fear of failure took hold of me.

At that time we played a game in Los Angeles, and Jan came up to be with me. We were staying in the Biltmore Hotel and Jan asked, "What in the world is wrong with you?" I had dropped twelve pounds in ten days and was so scared that I didn't know what to do. The problem was, I couldn't tell anybody that I was scared. If I did, then I would expose my weakness and lose control. I thought, *I'm a big leaguer, man. I've got to be tough.*

When Jan asked, "What's wrong?" I took a deep breath and confessed, "Honey, I'm scared to death. I don't know that I can pitch here. I think I've made a mistake. Everyone looks like Babe Ruth."

"I didn't marry you because you were a baseball player," she replied. "I don't care, for my sake, whether you stay in the big leagues or not. But you can pitch here just as well as you ever did. Why did they call you up? They called you up because you have what it takes. Don't try to be someone bigger or better. Why don't you just go out there and be you? Don't try to be somebody else!"

That's basically what was happening. I was so afraid that Dave Dravecky wasn't good enough that I was trying to change everything that got me to the big leagues in the first place. But Jan said, "Just go out there and be you. Use the stuff that got you here, and if that doesn't work, we'll go home! I don't care if we have to go back to Hawaii where you were playing AAA baseball; we were having a great time there."

Being able to admit my fear and hear my wife say that she loved me for myself, not for what I could do on the mound, freed me. Do you know how much pressure was released when I realized that my wife didn't give a rip whether I was wearing a big league uniform or not? A lot. Do you know how freeing it was to have a wife to whom I could say, "Honey, I am scared! I am afraid, and the fear of failure is killing me," and have her accept me and affirm her love for me? That was one of the most freeing experiences I've ever had.

The next night I couldn't wait for the bull pen phone to ring, with manager Dick Williams on the other end instructing Dave Dravecky to get up to pitch. When he did call, I was my old self again. I almost got my first major league win that night. I went on from that point and stayed in the big leagues for almost eight years. The moment I was able to release my fear, things started to fall into place. I discovered that admitting fear releases pressure.

It's just too bad I forgot that lesson the moment I left the ballpark.

What Do I Have to Say to Them?

I didn't admit weakness again for a long time. With two strong individuals like Jan and myself, it's easy to put your security in yourself. Jan and I had always been capable of taking care of ourselves. If there was something we wanted, we went after it. We didn't need (or ask for) anyone else's help.

After the amputation we continued in that self-sufficient mode. I'd go out on road trips and genuinely try to help people, though I was burning myself out. Of course I wouldn't admit it, but my fatigue showed up in the harsh way I was treating my family. For some reason I didn't understand why that was happening. Why was I one way out on the speaker circuit and a totally different way back home?

After one week of a lot of traveling and speaking, I came home to find a ton of work on my desk, representing all kinds of human needs. Mail and papers were stacked in a pile that seemed several feet high. Do you know how I responded to those needs? I planted my arm on the left side of the desk, swept it to the right, and, Woosh! no more piles. I don't remember if I was screaming or not. I do remember thinking, *I can't respond to these people. What do I have to say to them?*

I also took it out on the kids. When I came home, Jonathan would want to do something but I would tell him, "No, I'm too tired, leave me alone. I'm just not ready to go out and play. Go find a friend and play." Or I'd scream, "Why isn't this done right? Why isn't that put away? How come you don't have this hung up yet? This thing has been sitting here for a whole week. Last week before I left, I said to myself, 'Just watch, that thing is going to sit there for the entire week; and when I come back from this road trip, it will still be there.' And I was right! It's still there!" I'd go ballistic. It didn't take much, either, to get me going.

I'd also go on cleaning binges—and when I cleaned, you had better stay clear. I was neurotic about it (okay, I still am). When I'm tired, I can't stand for things to be less than perfect. Sometimes when I come home from a road trip, I can't help but pick out everything left undone. I look at all the jobs I have yet to do. I'm getting better, but I still struggle with this issue.

Jan has learned to handle it by saying, "Kids, it's time for us to leave. Father's cleaning, so let him scrub his area and we'll go do our thing." Then everybody splits, and there I am in the front yard cleaning, or out in the garage pushing the broom. That's part of my release. I can't get the kids or even Jan involved because then, in my mind, it becomes a mess. I don't want a mess; I want perfection. I still can be a cleaning freak, but at least we have more of a handle on it today than we did a few years back.

Worn Out at Our Own Game

What do you think of my household of just a few years ago? Not a very pretty picture, is it? I think now that a good portion of this happened because I was unwilling to admit weakness. When I go back in my mind and look at every situation where I blew up, I discover that my anger usually came out of frustra-tion, and the frustration came out of being tired. So what does that tell me? I'm not Superman. But I used to think I was.

I think God just allowed us to wear ourselves out at our own game. Eventually we cried out, "We can't do it anymore, we can't!" We had no strength left. We reached the point where we didn't give a rip; we didn't care what happened. When we were totally at the end of ourselves, when we had nothing left to give—that's when it got exciting, because that's when we saw the hand of God come in to provide his care. You could almost hear him say it: "*Now* you two have got it. It's never been you. I just let you two run out of steam. Now watch me put your life back together!"

When we were humbled and admitted our weakness, that's when we finally began to understand our true need for God. And for the first time in our lives, we realized that we had always placed our security in ourselves rather than in God.

Sound familiar? For most of us men, it's easy to think that everything depends on us. We work hard and we're rewarded for it. We get a paycheck that is able to provide us with a home, clothing on our backs, food on the table, and necessities for the family. It's easy to feel that we are in control, that our security is in ourselves.

But when that gets pulled out from underneath us, we begin to wonder where our security really comes from. And that's where God steps in.

When we are brought to the end of ourselves and admit our weakness, there is a release. When we finally realize how weak we are and that the power and the responsibility lies in God, not us; when we confess that the battle is the Lord's, not ours—that releases us and frees us from the responsibility of having to be perfect, of having to do it all.

But it's difficult, too, to rely on God. I won't deny it. It's a scary thing to put things in his hands when you're used to doing everything yourself. Yet I think if Jan and I hadn't been brought to the point of total weakness, we would never have known how much we could trust God and how faithful he is.

I always thought I had to hold on to God, as if it were up to me to keep the relationship going. When all of the hard things came into my life, one by one, I started thinking, *I can't hold on to you, God! I'm going to lose it altogether!* And then I fell—and guess where I fell? Straight into his hands! He had everything under control all the time. It didn't depend on me after all. What joy there is in that discovery!

I finally realized it was okay to be me. I didn't have to put on a costume that was something other than Dave Dravecky. I could be just me, with all my weaknesses and flaws, and that was okay. What a relief it was to finally rip that big "S" off my chest!

May I Help You?

In admitting my weakness, I finally found strength. I discovered that the often-quoted adage, "God helps those who help themselves," is not in the Bible (although a lot of people think it is). On the other hand, I found that 2 Corinthians 12:9–10 *is* in the Bible: "Therefore I will boast all the more gladly about my weaknesses, so that Christ's power may rest on me. . . . For when I am weak, then I am strong." I had to admit not only that I was weak, but also that I needed help.

A woman once told me a joke: How do we know that Moses was a man? Because he wandered forty years in the wilderness and never once stopped to ask for directions. She thought it was funnier than I did. She was laughing at the fact that many men seem willing to go to almost any length to avoid having to ask for help. I don't know if it's a part of our culture or a part of our nature, but I know from personal experience that asking for help is about the last thing I want to do.

As an amputee, I need help more often than a guy with a full set of limbs. There are a lot of little things I can't do for myself anymore, things like tying my shoes. Even though I accept the fact that I now face challenges that call for help, it is not much easier now than it ever was to admit I need help. My shoulder, arm, and hand may be gone, but in my mind I'm still a jock. I'm a pretty self-sufficient guy; I'm an athlete; I'm a well-trained fighting machine. I want to believe I can make it on my own.

One time I was trying to put my pants on and Jan just sat there watching. I knew that she wanted to help, but I wouldn't let her because I had to put my own pants on. Whenever I board an airplane carrying my hanging bag, I still make elaborate plans to figure out how I can hoist that bag into the overhead compartment without having to ask somebody for help. How do I do this without having to succumb to asking, "Would you please help me?" There's no way!

One of my greatest challenges in character development is admitting that I need help and that I will continue to need help. I need help in most ways: from the smallest thing like asking someone to tie my shoes or letting someone cut my meat, to the emotional adjustments Jan and I made with the help of a counselor. When I finally came to grips with the fact that, sooner or later, I'd have to ask somebody for help, I passed a marker on the road to maturity.

It freed me when both Dr. Dobson and Dr. Townsend told me point blank that I needed help. I don't know why I needed someone to give me permission to ask for help, but having other men I respect tell me that everybody needs help encouraged me tremendously. When I reached the end of my rope, I finally said, "I don't care what anybody thinks of me at this point. I need help!" And you know what? I got it.

Beginning the Communication Process

In order to admit your weaknesses you've got to verbalize them. And in verbalizing them, you begin the communication process. Once you're willing to admit your weaknesses, it becomes much easier to discuss openly what's going on in your life. Admitting your weaknesses leads to being much more open to talking about your life and your struggles.

When I agreed to go to counseling, Dr. Townsend recommended a therapist in our area. I went in with a lot of apprehension. I thought, *You're going to have to gain my trust, buddy, so you'd better be on guard!* When we got in there, at first all I did was listen. Jan was hurting so much that she ended up dominating most of the sessions. I told myself I was there for my wife. But as I saw it work with her, I became more open to the positive effect counseling could have on me. And as I said, within three weeks I was the one on the couch!

Counseling did something very simple for me: It taught me to be a better communicator. By learning how to listen and communicate, I was then able to identify and verbalize how I was feeling deep down inside. I learned to process with my wife what was going on inside, my feelings and thoughts. That let us become more supportive of each other. As Jan and I learned to understand each other and communicate our feelings, every part of our relationship got better.

In that counselor's office I found neutral ground, not threatening territory. It was great to have an arbitrator. I could say whatever I truly thought and felt without having to worry about it going anywhere else. That freed me to say what was on my heart.

Jan and I have learned a lot about weakness, and we're still learning. One thing we've learned is that admitting weakness is a key step toward understanding our true worth. Only when everything was stripped away did we come to see that our truth worth comes from the One who has created us. Without admitting our weakness, we never would have found the right path.

Recently Jan has been reading a devotional called *Let God*, taken from the writings of the archbishop of Canterbury to the court of King Louis XIV. It contains a great quote that sums up what we've learned about weakness so far. I'd like to reproduce it here as an excellent way to close this chapter.

> I'm amazed at the power that comes to us through suffering. We are nothing without the cross. Of course I tremble and agonize while it lasts, and all my words about the beneficial effects of suffering vanish under the torture, but when it is all over, I look back over on the experience with deep appreciation and am ashamed that I bore it with so

much bitterness. I am learning a great deal from my own foolishness.[1]

Notes

1. Archbishop of Canterbury, *Let Go* (Springdale, Pa: Whitaker House, 1973), p. 5.

Chapter Four

You Mean I Have to Talk?

It has always been difficult for me to communicate, which is ironic when you realize that I now travel all over the country, speaking and sharing my story with others.

I think a lot of my struggle to communicate stems from my childhood. As much as mom and dad may have tried to get me to talk, I was rarely able to open up and let them know what was going on inside. That, to a great extent, has carried over into my adult life. Communication continues to be a struggle for me—in fact, it's probably one of the toughest challenges I face. Yet if you don't communicate, you can pretty well count on struggling with issues of personal worth throughout your life.

Learning to Release

Jan and I were in counseling for sixteen months in Ohio. It was there I finally began to learn the basics of good communication. I think I had to go through a period in the first stage of counseling where I dealt with releasing all the things that were bugging me. In Ohio we dealt with our struggles, with the problems, with identifying our weaknesses.

The setting of our counseling was especially conducive to getting me to communicate; I felt safe there. Jan would name something I had done or said, then the counselor would look at me and say, "Now, Dave, how do you feel about this? Did you do that? Did you say that?" And I would defend myself and begin to talk about the situation. It forced communication between Jan and me. The tools for communicating were given to me by the example set in our counseling sessions.

When we moved to Colorado Springs, we obviously broke loose from our counseling in Ohio. About four or five months after the move, we got connected with Gary Oliver, a wonderfully helpful counselor in Littleton, Colorado. By then my communication skills had developed significantly. The first thing Gary said to me was, "Dave, we're here to bring resolution to your problems. We want you out of this place in a short period of time. You've already identified your weaknesses, so we don't have to go over all of that again. You already know why you feel like you do. So let's get on with it. Let's move on."

Gary was "solution based." In our sessions we moved from identifying the problems to figuring out a way to resolve them. At this point I began dealing with my weaknesses and recognizing that in my weakness I can be strong.

I quickly discovered that the only way to bring resolution to any situation is to respond to the questions being asked of me. In other words, I *had* to talk. I had no choice if I wanted to resolve the problem and the struggle I was facing. While I don't remember the specific questions, I do know that I ended up saying a lot that I never intended to say!

Pleasing God Rather Than Man

An important discovery that has helped make it possible for me to resolve my struggles was that I didn't have to live up to other people's expectations. I learned that God loved me, period. True, even he has certain expectations of me, but they have no bearing on whether he will love me. He just does. That was very freeing to me, to the point where I thought, *Okay, there's no condition here.* It had a major impact on my under-standing of my worth as a man.

Yet I am the first to admit that this discovery isn't always lived out in my life. Both Jan and I struggle with pleasing other people rather than God. Our time with Gary Oliver was espe-cially beneficial to us in that we began learning how to listen to the voice of God. When you know that you're walking according to God's leading, you find the strength to stand against human expectations. That's what we've been learning over the past two years. We've learned to go to God in prayer, hear his voice, find his leading, and then stand in our decision and withstand all the repercussions it may bring.

But we're not always good at that. Jan and I are both sensi-tive, our feelings are easily hurt, and we sometimes say yes when perhaps we should say no. In the old days before we learned about boundaries and listening to God's voice, we said yes to everyone because we didn't want to hurt their feelings. Since then we have found that by saying no, we have offended lots of people, many of whom became angry at us. That has been hard for us to deal with, and sometimes it still causes us to be unwilling to do the right thing.

For example, this year I took a trip where I committed to speak four times in two days. Now, why would I do that after my experience in California, where I spoke eight times in five days in four cities? Well, for one thing, I was tired when I said yes. For another, I didn't want to disappoint the people who asked me to speak. And I ended up paying for it.

The point is, it's one thing to say that we're creating bound-aries by listening to God's voice; it's another to admit that those boundaries seem to change all the time. We cannot say, "We've got the answers now and everything's cool. Here we go on this wonderful ride of life, this fantasy dream of happiness. No more problems!" We're not there. But I can assure you that in these last five years I have learned a lot about where I should be and the journey I should be on. And that's a big, big step in the right direction.

In listening to God's voice and in understanding my true worth before God, I now see that I don't have to live up to people's expectations. I am responsible to God. I am still learning and I still make mistakes, but I am going to keep pressing ahead. After all, none of the other alternatives lead anywhere I'd like to be (see Philippians 3:12–14).

The Struggle Continues

Even after learning so much about communication and seeing how it benefits me and my family, it is an ongoing struggle for me. I don't understand why I can be so open and vulnerable with strangers, but then come home and clam up with Jan or the kids.

There are logical reasons for some of it, of course. Frankly, when you're a speaker, it's tiring to communicate "out there" and then come home and realize that you have to continue communication "back here." That's been a tough thing for me; I do it well sometimes and badly at other times.

Jan and I have found that our best time to talk is at night. If we get to bed early enough, we can sit and discuss important issues. Sometimes we're so exhausted that we both crash. But there are also times when we talk, and those are good times. A lot of helpful things come out of such conversations.

Sometimes we take a trip to get away. It's not uncommon that on the first day we don't speak much to each other. We've been so busy talking during the course of our regular routine that we need a break. I mean, that's what I get paid to do—speak. Jan also speaks to groups periodically, and all day long she's talking to people on the phone for the ministry. So when we get out, we need a day of silence.

But after that, we start talking. We'll start discussing how we can spend more time with each other, what we're going to do in devotional times, or how we are going to relate to the kids. A lot of times our conversation revolves around Tiffany and Jonathan because we are concerned about the legacy we're leaving to them. What kind of message are we sending to them? That is really important to us.

Yet I know how short I come in that area. I have a long way to go when it comes to communicating with my kids. I have had to learn from the ground floor up with both of them. It's tough for me to ask them questions because I tend to react first and then ask. I don't easily sit and listen, though I think I'm making good strides in that area.

Jan has helped me here. She's my coach. She will say to me, "Dave, you really need to go to your daughter and tell her you're sorry," or "You really need to go to Jonathan and apologize for what you just did."

This never happened until I began to understand the value of being honest and admitting when I've done wrong. I can't tell you how many times I've had to say "I'm sorry" to Tiffany and Jonathan. How many kids all over this country would love to hear something like that from their parents? "I don't know" or "I messed up and I'm sorry" are absent from the vocabulary of far too many parents. That's sad. I know this has been a valuable part of our family relationship.

I have found that our children are more ready to admit that they have done wrong when I've apologized to them for some wrong I did to them. That has been a real lesson for me in the value of communicating and in being vulnerable as a man, though it has not been an easy lesson. I find I need a lot of refresher courses.

In addition to that, in counseling both Jan and I have learned how to find and enjoy healthy relationships with friends. That too has been important for us. Not only did we have to understand that God accepted us just as we are, but it was also necessary for our friends to accept us where we were at. So it has been great to find a group of people who really do understand.

Bob Knepper was a pitcher for the Houston Astros who was traded to the San Francisco Giants just before I made my comeback in August of 1989. We played on the same team for five days, until I fell from the mound. Since then we haven't played baseball together, but we have become good friends. He and his wife, Teri, live nearby. Bob had been out of the game for two and a half years when we moved to Colorado Springs. He was dealing with some of the same issues I was, so he could understand and empathize with my struggles. Ken and Judy Gire, who are really close to us (Ken was my co-author on *When You Can't Come Back*; Judy wrote *A Boy and His Baseball*, a kids' book about my story), can also understand, for they too have gone through some of the same things. Rock Bottomly, our former pastor, and his wife, Bev, gave us spiritual direction and insight as we battled our struggles. We have been fortunate to find a group of core people who understand and are supportive and encouraging as we walk through our life.

Good communication is equally important in man-to-man friendships. When I am able to open up and communicate what's going on inside of me with another man, and his response says, "I care about your struggle. I'm here to help. I don't have all the answers, but because I care, I want you to know that I'll be with you through it," it really does help me to sense my worth in God's eyes.

Communication With God

It's important to communicate with each other that our worth is in who we are, not what we do, because whenever we start thinking our worth is tied up in what we do, we can get down on ourselves. For example, my prayer life is not as good as I would like it to be. I used to bind myself up with the fact that I was not in the prayer closet an hour a day. But Richard Foster's book on prayer has been helpful to me. He was honest about his struggles with prayer. He'd say things like, "Sometimes I pray and I don't get any answer back. Why? Have I done something wrong? Or at other times I just don't feel like praying."

I could relate to that because there have been many times I didn't feel like praying. But that doesn't mean I lack a desire to communicate with God. Ultimately, I do desire to communicate with my heavenly Father. I have a burning desire to communicate with him, and through learning how to communicate with my wife, kids, and friends, that desire has grown. It has become deeper. I have a longing to want to talk to God about what's going on in my life. I've gotten beyond the point of bogging myself down in wondering whether he's hearing me and whether he's going to respond to me.

Because I'm communicating with God, I can grow much closer in my relationship with him. I don't understand the dynamics of it, but I do know that along with this desire is a tremendous peace and contentment in my relationship with him when I am talking to him. It's easier to admit my weaknesses. I suppose that's confession—the willingness to be open and honest before him.

Honesty Before God

A neat thing happens when I'm honest and transparent with God. In some way, by being honest with him, I connect with his love for me as my heavenly Father. And to be honest, that's a hard thing for me to do. It's probably one of the greatest struggles I have, outside of communication itself. I still wonder sometimes, *Does God really love me?* And on the flipside of that, I wonder, *How do I respond in love to him?* In ways I don't understand, being open and honest with him helps me to connect with all that.

I suppose this shouldn't be too surprising. I know how much my parents appreciated my being honest about the times I messed up as a kid. I remember, for example, a trip I took with some of my buddies. We were driving age, seventeen or eighteen years old, and my dad let us take his Ford station wagon. We were driving on a muddy and slippery path to get to our campsite and I stepped on the gas. All of a sudden, "Boom!"— the car fishtailed into a tree. I put a big dent in the rear right quarter panel.

As we continued driving along, a low-hanging tree limb clipped off the antenna. Now I had a smash in the back and a broken antenna. Yet that night I decided, along with the other guys, to drink. Well, I got drunk. I climbed in my dad's car and started doing fishtails in the field, where I ran over a tree trunk and stripped the muffler completely off the car.

The next day we clanked into Boardman, Ohio, and I pulled up to the front curb of my house. I didn't want to pull into the driveway because the car sounded as if it was falling apart. When my dad heard an odd but loud noise, he came from the backyard where they were swimming, looked at his beat-up car, and asked, "What in the world did you guys do?" He pulled my brother and I into the house and asked me point blank, "Dave, did you guys get drunk while you were out there?" I replied, "Yes, we did. We were drinking." Meanwhile my brother was standing next to me and whispering, "You jerk! Why did you tell him we were drinking?!" I figured it was better to be honest since the punishment was going to be a lot worse if I wasn't.

Because I was honest, my dad responded in a gentle way. Oh, we did get punished. We were grounded for the weekend and weren't allowed to go anywhere, see anybody, or do anything. But, we deserved it. That day I saw a loving father in my dad, who responded to us out of both mercy and justice.

Somehow I can't help but think that, in some small way, that is how God responds to us as our loving Father when we find ourselves coming home in less than mint condition. All of that comes from communication, from being open and honest about who we are and what we have done. Through communication I am learning it's okay to be me. I want to be real before other people. I don't want to be one way here and then something totally different over there. I want what you see to be what you get.

You know why? Because that's a truth that sets people free. God can handle whatever you and I are going through. If your friends or your church can't handle it, I say, find those who can. Don't give up being real to try to please people. It's better, if necessary, to give up the people who don't want you to be real. Finding people who will affirm you when you are honest about your struggles is a difficult task. But it's a task well worth pursuing. And you might be surprised at the discoveries you make if you give it a try.

Right and Wrong Ways to Communicate

It has been helpful to me to realize that communication can take many forms, both constructive and destructive. It's one thing to say, "It's good to communicate." But frankly, anyone can communicate; we do it all the time. We communicate in the office when we berate a fellow employee who did something that upset us. We communicate on the ball field after we strike out or give up a home run. But it's another thing to learn to communicate the right way, to build people up rather than tear them down. I'm beginning to learn that not only is it important to express what's going on inside of me, but that *how* I express myself also communicates a message to those I love.

There's a major difference between communicating out of frustration over what my kids or wife have done and communicating out of love. This was a crucial thing for me to understand, because it is difficult for me to readily feel any emotion except anger. Anger is one of my major problems. It's not as if I shout all the time, but when I go off, you don't want to be around. You're about to see what I mean.

Chapter Five

How to Ground Flying Furniture

I received quite a shock the first time I looked in the mirror after my amputation. I don't know what I expected, but when I saw nothing where my pitching arm and shoulder used to be, it didn't register. Immediately, I minimized my loss by comparing it with the greater losses of other people in the cancer ward where I was a patient. I told myself, *Look, Dravecky, you lost your arm; there are people within your reach who are losing their wives, their children, their very lives.*

I did not deal with my loss. Instead, I turned to helping others worse off than I was. That activity allowed me to sidestep the full impact of what I had seen in the mirror. I realize now that I was in shock and denial, which is a normal part of adjusting to an amputation. But God was able to work, even through that, to help others. There was value in giving of myself to other people, even though it served as an initial distraction. The bottom line, however, was that I encouraged others in order to separate me from my own pain.

Whenever I speak, I usually show a video recapping my baseball career, my cancer, my comeback, the fall from the mound, and the amputation of my arm. I have watched people in the audience cry, mourning the loss of something precious. One day I realized they were crying for *me*. They were shedding tears over my loss—something I wasn't doing. I didn't feel anything. People came up to me and talked about the struggles associated with losing a career and letting go of dreams. They assumed I was in touch with all of that, but I wasn't. I was disconnected from my own sense of loss.

I was afraid to deal with the feelings associated with losing my career because I didn't want to expose the strong feelings inside me that I didn't think should be there. I was unwilling to let people see I was hurting deep down inside over the loss of a game I loved so much. Somehow, it didn't seem like the Christian thing to do. It didn't seem right to say how deeply I missed baseball, that I loved the game and everything it meant to me. It didn't seem "spiritual" to admit that when I lost my arm and the game of baseball with it, I lost my identity, that I had to give up all my unfulfilled goals, that I had to accept I'd never win in a World Series or pitch a no-hitter. Those dreams were real to me. I thought that to admit how much those losses hurt would be like saying baseball was my god and that God wasn't big enough to fill my loss.

As a result, I pent all of that up inside . . . and four months later I was in depression. Allen Redpath has said, "When God wants to do an impossible thing, he takes an impossible man and crushes him." The pent-up emotions crushed me from the inside out. Yet God never required that I pretend to be fine; that was my own misconception. God didn't force me to grieve my losses, either. He just let me go on until the illusion faded and reality won out.

For awhile I thought I was doing a pretty good job of burying my pain and sense of loss. I was proud of how well I was doing by not feeling anything. I have since learned that it takes more strength to face our losses squarely and feel the pain than it does to avoid our losses and disconnect from our feelings. But back then, I knew none of this.

At some point God withdrew the emotional anesthesia and allowed the real hurt to sink in. He brought me to a place where I was really being crushed by the realization that I had no clue who I was anymore. I became tired of saying and not feeling, "My identity is in Christ." I became tired of saying and not feeling, "I am a child of God." I believed these things intellectually, but I just couldn't feel them. My heart grew cold—even to God—because when you deaden yourself to pain and loss, you can't feel anything else either.

The spiritual surgery began when I decided to deal with what was *really* going on inside me instead of what I thought was *supposed* to be going on. Only when I admitted how much I missed baseball, my career, my friends, my lost hopes and dreams, did God help me to get beyond my losses to a new sense of identity. The road of sorrows that ran through the valley of suffering is where I finally began to see who I am and what my life is really worth.

Anger Comes From Somewhere

Stuffing my feelings inside and refusing to recognize them not only kept me from understanding my worth as a man, it also led to another unpleasant consequence: uncontrolled anger. When I refused to face up to what was going on inside me, eventually it came out anyway in the form of anger.

A lot of guys I know struggle with trying to control their anger. My own anger used to get out of control, especially before I became a Christian. My temper scared me because I could not get a handle on it.

I can recall one particularly bad occasion when I was at the top of my game and puffed up with a sense of my own self-importance. It was 1986, we were in San Diego, our team was winning, and I felt invincible. I placed tremendous expectations both on myself and on Jan. I figured that if I could keep on top of my game, she could certainly keep our home in perfect order. Our kids were small—Tiffany was five and Jonathan two. And we all know how easy it is to keep the house in order with two active preschool kids under foot, right? Ha!

I had just finished a road trip and came home tired. I expected my wife, children, and home to be in perfect order when I returned. I walked in and saw towels lying on the bathroom floor. I saw pillows on the bedroom floor and stuff left out on the bathroom counter. I went to the kitchen and saw a few things out of place down there as well. I was growing angry because the house was not in order, and I was reaching the boiling point.

I yelled at Jan, "Why is it so hard to take your towel and put it on the stinkin' rack after you've taken a shower? What is wrong with you?"

I had created such high expectations for my wife that she was broken by them. Well, she must have had enough that day. I was raging around the house, bellowing in my usual way, spewing out my anger. Finally she glared at me and said, "I am sick and tired of trying to live up to your expectations! I have had it!"

"*You've* had it?" I raged. "You've had it! Fine—I really don't care anymore. I don't care if this towel is on the floor." I grabbed the towels and threw them on the floor. "I don't care if the clothes are on the floor." I went into the closet and grabbed armful after armful of clothes and threw them all over. The bed was nicely made; I ripped the covers off, lifted up the mattress and threw it off its box springs. By this time the children were cowering in Jan's arms, but I wasn't finished. I walked over to the armoire and threw it crashing to the floor.

Oh, I felt like such a powerful guy. I looked up and saw my two little kids in my wife's lap, crying in fear of their raging father. Yet even that didn't stop me. I went into the hallway, started grabbing towels out of the cupboard, and threw them over the balcony into the living room. All the while, I was screaming. "I don't care if it's a mess! If you don't care, I don't care!"

When my rage was spent, Jonathan and Tiffany sat there, cringing in their mother's arms and looking at me as if I was a raving maniac (which I guess I was). The look of fear in their eyes stopped me in my tracks. How I wish I had stopped sooner! Today I see Jonathan struggling to control his anger, and I think, *Oh God, what have I done? Where does this stop? It has to stop with me!*

Sadly, we men seem to lack an acceptable vocabulary to discuss hurt, frustration, and fear. How many guys do you know who sit around and talk about the hurt they are feeling or what makes them afraid? It's not acceptable to talk about such feelings; if you do, you sound like a whiner. On the other hand, anger is an acceptable emotion. Just let somebody bring up the subject of what ticks him off, and everybody in the room will have something to add.

Help for Anger

For me, a good part of learning to communicate has been discovering how to control my anger. It doesn't take a genius to figure out that when you're raging around the house, not a lot of positive communication is going on.

Gary Oliver taught us how to communicate when I was angry. I learned how to step back from my anger, look at what was causing it, discover the reasons for it, and then communicate what I found. It's usually when things aren't communicated that I blow. Gary helped me to see that there are reasons why my anger builds, but I won't discover them unless I communicate.

So much of anger can be eliminated if there is an open line of communication about what is going on inside us. Today if I express my frustration by saying something like, "I'm getting real frustrated with this and I need some time," I usually get the time and the space I need.

Sometimes, however, I'm not able to get to that place where I express my frustration, hurt, or fear. From time to time it builds to the point of anger, and then I release the anger. If for a period of time I haven't been talking about the struggles I've been having—and these things may have nothing to do with my relationship with Jan or my kids—so often *my family members* end up being the ones on the receiving end of my anger. I had to have a way of dealing with this.

The Anger Curve

Gary Oliver gave me a way of dealing with anger. He introduced me to what he calls "The Anger Curve." He draws a curved arch and along the ascending line writes, "hurt, frustration, fear." At the height of the arch goes the word "anger." He then explains how many people (including me) don't register much, if any, emotional connection with their hurt, frustration, and fear. They don't feel anything until they get to the point of anger. Once many guys become angry, they may be unable to stop their heated outbursts.

This tool showed me how to track the origins of my rising anger back to hurt, frustration, or fear, and to identify how close I am to the top of the curve. I don't write out this curve every time I feel anger coming on, but I've learned to ask myself: *Why am I angry? Is this anger growing out of frustration, or fear, or hurt?*

For example, I have a hard time putting on my pants with one arm. I don't like it, nor the feeling of helplessness it causes. One day I was struggling to get my pants on and Jan was sitting right there. I kept trying and could feel the anger rising. By understanding and using the anger curve, I was able to realize, *I am getting really frustrated right now and if somebody doesn't step in and help me, I'm going to blow!* In that situation I didn't blow up. I could deal with my frustration by saying, "Hey, Honey, I'm getting really frustrated here. Do you think you could help me?" Believe me, Jan appreciates that far more than an angry tirade.

Understanding anger helps me identify other feelings inside of me. When I feel anger coming on, I try to pull away and ask, "Why is this happening? Am I afraid at this point? No. Am I hurt? No. Am I frustrated? You better believe I am. Okay. I'll deal with the underlying emotion." By doing this over a period of time, my anger has become more manageable.

This anger curve can also be used to help our kids learn to deal with their own anger. The Bible says that we should be angry and yet not sin, that we should not let the sun go down on our anger. That means we must resolve our anger. And I think we also have an obligation to help our children resolve their anger in healthy ways.

As I said, Jonathan has a temper like mine: hot. I used to overpower his anger with my own, but that didn't go very far toward helping him find a healthy resolution. Now I try to sit down with him and say, "Hey, why are you angry? Have you been hurt?"

"No."

"Are you frustrated?"

"Yeah!"

"Why?"

"Well, somebody [usually his sister] has been giving me a hard time."

Then we talk about the underlying reason for his anger. Guess what? In the ten minutes that we talk about his frustration, he's forgotten about throwing fits. This is a lesson I am trying to teach my son even while practicing it myself. It's helping our whole family.

Identifying and Defusing the Anger

I'm so grateful that God is helping me get my anger under control much more than it ever was, though I still have to watch out that it doesn't build to the blow-up point. On a practical level, that means I have to learn what contributes to the buildup of my anger and then learn to defuse it. It means admitting that outbursts of anger are sin—to be confessed, repented of, and not excused or tolerated.

It seems easiest to blow up at home when you're used to being the big shot at work. In the major leagues, even as a Christian, I sometimes let my status go to my head. I realized that all the attention I got came because I was a major league baseball player. Then I came home and expected everybody to jump at my commands.

Even though I haven't been in baseball for several years now, this is still true for me. A lot of attention is still directed toward Dave Dravecky. At times I have allowed myself to be puffed up by the honors, offers, and opportunities I have received—everything from writing books to going to the White House to meet the president. I think God gives us our families to deflate us and shrink us back down to size, so that we are bearable.

You know what happens when I go home after feeling pretty self-important? After three or four days where I've been puffed up by all kinds of people, I go home and act like a bear. At the drop of a hat, I'll yell at the normal things my kids do. For example, I have a ten-year-old who tends to sit at the table with about three feet between his mouth and his plate. Somehow he hauls food across this great divide, spilling about half of it. I don't just correct him, I get irate: "Sit in your chair, pull it up to the table, and eat properly!"

Most of the time, his eating habits don't bother me; but when I'm tired and I've just come off a trip where well-meaning people have been giving me all kinds of attention, I think, *Now I have to put up with this? I don't think so!* It's both maddening and humbling to have a stand-off with a child who is oblivious to the fact that you are a big shot.

The Transition Home

The transition from work to home isn't easy. In my situation, people usually treat me as someone special; it feels so good, but it creates something inside that makes me feel bigger than I really am. The Bible says that love is not puffed up. Whenever I let myself get puffed up, there is greater danger of a blowup.

Counseling has helped me deal with the transition between work and home. One of the things I've learned is to consciously make the transition while I'm on the way back to the ranch. I think about my family, their concerns, what's going on at school, and what issues they may have been dealing with while I was at work. I begin to deflate myself and get out of that arena in which I had all the power and received all the attention. In other words, I consciously bring myself back down to reality.

One of my friends has a long drive between work and home. He spends the first part of his drive hashing over all the stuff he's carrying with him from work. Mentally he puts it all in an imaginary bag and tosses it out the window at a particular freeway cutoff. The rest of the drive he thinks about each member of his family and rehearses what he wants to do with them and talk about with them when he gets home. Then on the way back to work he picks up the mental bag where he dropped it off and carries his work-related thoughts to the office with him.

In the same way, I have to remind myself that I'm not going to be a celebrity when I get home. I am a husband and a father, loving and serving my family. I know I don't succeed all the time; but at least I've progressed to where I make a consistent effort. With God's help, I'm doing much better than I was. I realize now that if I succeed in my profession but lose my family in the process, being the center of attention isn't worth a thing.

It's Also Less Expensive

I'm sure I'll continue to wrestle with anger all along my journey, but I'm improving. I haven't thrown furniture in a long time. I have thrown phones, but no furniture. That's made life much more enjoyable for everyone, and it's helped me to better live out my God-given worth as a man. Oh yes, and one other thing:

It's a whole lot less expensive (even though the furniture companies probably don't think that's such a great thing).

Chapter Six

First Things First

One of the chief reasons I have had such a hard time coming to understand my worth as a man has been my tendency to doubt whether God could really love me. No, that's not exactly right. I've always believed he *could* love me; I've just doubted whether he *did*.

It's one thing to accept truth intellectually; it's quite another to get it into your heart. I know that God is God and he is who he says he is. I know what he's done for us through the death of his Son on the cross. But I've struggled to connect with this affection that God insists he has for me, to understand his unconditional love, and to respond back in love. I don't know how to do that very well.

I Love My Kids

Thank God, at least one thing is helping me to bridge this gap: I know I love my own kids. Whenever I think about something bad happening to them, I get a knot in the pit of my stomach. Even when something less dramatic than my imaginations does happen to them—when they get sick or when they hurt themselves—I get a deep pain in my heart. It devastates me.

I don't think it's an exaggeration to say that I love my kids so much that I'd die for them. I hate to think what I'd do to the person who tried to harm them. I don't see how I could ever exchange one of their lives for the life of someone else—yet that's exactly what God did for us.

When I think about that and about what Scripture says of the love of God for me, it becomes a little easier to accept the fact that he really does love me. If I can love my own children with such passion, then how much more is he who is perfect able to love me?

In this way, I have come to better understand and accept God's love for me. That, in turn, has helped me to glimpse something of my worth as a man.

When They Sin, Do You Still Love Them?

Such reflections have also helped me to realize that when my children fail, I don't love them any less. I look at one of my kids, sitting there in his or her own little world, bound and determined to do something despite what mom or dad might say. Do I love them any less because of it? Of course not. Sure, I'll get angry with them; but my love never disappears because of what they might do.

Moreover, it strikes me that as I look at a disobedient son or daughter, I see myself. I'm no different than Jonathan or Tiffany—I'm just a bigger, older version! I'm no different at all.

So what does that mean? Could it mean that God continues to love us despite our sins, just as we continue to love our kids despite theirs? Absolutely! God does not rejoice when I fall, nor does he rub his hands and say, "Aha! I told you so!" I find great comfort in that.

This thought has been a real eye-opener for me, because I tend to get down on myself whenever I fail miserably. I do not want to go to God at those times because I don't feel worthy. Yet that's when I need him more than at any other time.

When we sin terribly or fail according to our own standards, that's when most of us want to run away from God. We don't want to face him. Yet that's the time we most need to go before God. It helps me to think about my children. When they fail, I still love them. I hurt for them when they fail, and I hate the fact that they have to suffer the consequences of their sin, but I still love them. I've come to understand that God responds to us in the same way. He hates our sin and regrets the consequences that come to us because of our sin, but he doesn't love us any less. His love remains constant.

I love my kids. And I am beginning to see that God loves me as one of his kids, although in a much greater way than I ever could. My relationship with my kids is helping me to both better understand and connect with God's love for me personally. And it's also helping me to get a better grip on my worth as a man made in his image.

First Things First

I mention my struggle with accepting the love of God because it played such a big part in the counseling we received from the spring of 1994 to the spring of 1995 (we have great insurance coverage—you have to in baseball, the way the game drives people loony!). Part of my problem was that I had allowed the expectations and demands of people to cloud my understanding of how God saw and accepted me. Jan had the same problem. Remember, both of us were performance-driven people; as long as we performed, we felt loved. But as soon as we let people down by not performing up to their expectations, we felt less "lovable" and less "worthy," both in their eyes and in God's eyes. Our counselor spotted that problem and helped us to deal with it.

What probably helped us most was the concept of "first things first." We had life backwards, and Gary Oliver helped us get our priorities in order and put down boundaries in our lives. He used the phrase "first things first" to remind us that more important than anything we can *do* is realizing who we *are* before God because of what he has done for us. Out of that understanding comes our desire to have fellowship with him and serve him.

This idea has helped us to do a number of things. For one, I am not involved in every good ministry that's out there. God has given us a specific ministry that reaches out to cancer patients and amputees. We reach out and love these people where they are at, as Jesus loves them, with actions and not only with words. God has gifted us in certain areas and withheld gifts in many others. The trick for me has been to find those areas in which I am gifted and then use those talents, right where I am, to represent God.

The same is true for all of us. Our "calling" may be collecting garbage or writing or working in a factory—or being diagnosed with cancer and realizing you've been given an opportunity to minister to cancer patients. That's the place in life where God has put Jan and me. So we responded right where we were at and began reaching out to people in similar circumstances.

We discovered our niche only by connecting with this idea of "first things first." I first had to recognize where my priorities and gifts lay. That's true in all spheres of life, not just in ministry. And it isn't some mechanical thing; it's a simple fact of life.

For example, when I got married, I took on a responsibility to my wife. When I made that choice, God made it clear that my responsibility to her took precedence over many other things. "First things first" reminds me that after God comes my wife, then my children. I have a responsibility to my family before I have a responsibility to anybody outside my home. And from there I have a responsibility to the people with whom I come in contact every day, with those whom God sends my way. It wouldn't make any difference if I had a nonprofit ministry (as I do) or if I were out there in the work force connecting with people and meeting them in the place God had placed me. Wherever God has put me, that becomes the place of my ministry.

Once I understood that, I found a solid structure that helped relieve a lot of guilt and confusion about where we should be. "First things first" gave definition to what we should do with our lives. It gave us freedom to say no to some things because we knew we were saying yes to more important things.

The interesting thing is that when my life slows down and when I pace myself—when I know when to say no and when to say yes, when I'm giving to my family, when I'm devoting time to Jan, when I'm devoting time to my kids—I feel so much better in my relationship with God. I really do begin to sense my worth as a man.

God at the Center

As you break down this idea and apply it to other areas of life, you see that the question is not, "How do I fit God into everything that's going on in my life," but, "How do I fit all this stuff that's already in my life around God at the center?"

When Jan and I began to see life from the perspective of "first things first," we stopped trying to meet everybody's needs and demands. As we began to understand where all the demands of life fit into our lives in light of our commitment to God, we realized there was a whole lot of "stuff" that was just that: stuff, excess baggage. It was junk that didn't need to be there. So instead of pouring our energies into those things, we began focusing on the things that were most important in life. We began to put our efforts into those areas where God had gifted us. Only then did we begin to put things in perspective and to realize that even if some of those things fell away or disappeared, we still had incredible worth in our relationship with God.

Although this perspective frees us from trying to meet the expectations of others, that doesn't mean that God has no expectations of us. Certainly he does. I think the Bible is clear that he wants our lives to represent him, that he calls us to a life of obedience and holiness and worship. But what's crucial to recognize is that *his love for us never changes in the midst of that pursuit*. It never changes! Even when we mess up.

Lest you get the wrong impression, let me hasten to add that this idea of "first things first" hasn't solved all my problems. It's one thing to say that "first things first" reminds me to put my relationship with God first, then my relationship with Jan, then the kids, and then the ministry and the people I come into contact with. But it's quite another thing to say that it always works out that way in practice. One of my greatest struggles right now is trying to live by what I know to be true.

For example, I'd love to take out each of my kids, once a week. It's a great idea—but one I have yet to put into practice. Oh, periodically I take them on a trip with me, but the once-a-week-outing-with-Dad has yet to happen.

I'd also love to take out Jan on dates and spend more time alone with her, but to be honest with you, I've not done that as much as I think I should. We have managed a few of these dates. Neither of us cares a whole lot for a night on the town, so we're perfectly satisfied with having a date here at home. We put our kids to bed at 8:30 or 9:00 and nothing keeps us from sitting down in the jacuzzi, relaxing, and talking. That's what makes us happy; that's what satisfies. We both know that we need to get away periodically, but we're a little behind in that department.

So I have to keep working at "first things first"; I haven't mastered it yet, not by a long shot. But you know what? I'm not beating myself up anymore because of my shortcomings, and that's wonderful. I'm not loaded down with guilt because I fall short, and I'm not losing sight of what I know is important. My goals have remained clear through it all, and I'm pursuing them with all my heart. That's a huge change for me, and it's been terrific.

It hasn't been very long that I have been able to say without guilt, "Okay, God, I've messed up today. There's not a whole lot I can do about that. The day's gone. What am I going to do about tomorrow?" Sometimes after I mess up I'll wake up the next day and think, *I feel just as lousy today as I did yesterday*. It may be two or three days before I start "connecting" again with God, but that too is okay. I don't think God sits up there with a sledgehammer or two, getting ready to pound me with his divine hammer just because Dave isn't perfect.

Yet at the same time, I don't want to make it sound as if it's okay to be sloppy with life. Grace does not give me a license to sin, to do whatever I feel like doing. But it does give me the strength to carry on when I've messed up, as well as the courage to push further ahead in my walk with God today than I was with him yesterday.

Looking Back to Look Ahead

On June 18, 1991, I walked into the Sloan Kettering Cancer Research Hospital to have my left arm and shoulder removed. Four months later I went into depression. For the next sixteen months Jan and I went through counseling in Ohio. Shortly after that we moved to Colorado Springs and hooked up with Gary Oliver, where the second major phase of counseling began, learning to resolve the problems we had previously identified. That was a tremendously difficult three years, by any assessment. But I'll tell you the absolute truth: What we learned during that agonizing period has more than made up for the pain we had to endure.

When I say my ordeal has been a blessing in my life, people often give me the most bizarre looks. But who would have listened to me had my story not unfolded the way it did? I always wanted God to use me to get his message across to others; and let's face it, it is my pain and suffering that has attracted attention to my story. I don't think a lot of people would be listening to what Dave Dravecky has to say if everything had gone hunky-dory and I was making two to three million dollars a year. Few people can relate to that. If I had continued on as a baseball player who played his ten years, retired financially independent, and got on with life, who would have strained to hear what Dave Dravecky had to say? Not a whole lot of folks, outside of avid sports fans.

But when, by the grace of God, I was able to get through my ordeal, then people wanted to listen. Because of what God allowed me to go through, I can encourage others who are suffering. I don't take this lightly because I know how important faith and encouragement are when you or a loved one faces adversity.

Why do people listen to what I say now? I think it's more than just because I was a baseball player. God orchestrated events so that people were able to watch me hurt. They saw me come back from cancer; they saw me fall from the mound. I didn't orchestrate that. God used those circumstances to make me a better man and to reach out to others.

The troubles I have gone through have opened doors of hope to countless others who are suffering. I have had a chance to talk with people all over the world—in person, through books, and through other media—about the love of God and the true worth of a man. That's a tremendous privilege and a great honor. Yet it's been anything but a smooth ride.

This Roller-Coaster Ride Called Life

I have concluded that life is like a roller-coaster ride. Everybody—and I mean everybody—is going to face some tremendous ups and downs. We all are going to be forced into situations where we are on top one moment and headed down fast the next. Our identity changes, sometimes in ways we don't like. A man may be a husband one minute, a widower the next; a vice-president one day, a consultant the next; a pitcher one season, a one-armed man the next. Life doesn't request our permission to make changes. It just changes and we have to adjust.

A friend of mine named Rick knows the drill. "I'm a film editor," he told me. "I make good money when I work, but the business is unpredictable even for those of us who are established. A while back, I was unemployed for six months between projects. When our savings ran low, we had to depend on God and the goodness of our friends to get us through. I doubted myself. But I saw miracles, too. When I finally got back to work, I found myself encouraging another man who was laid off. I didn't give him answers. I just described how I felt when I was going through it. I felt the same self-doubt, the same fears, as he did. I offered little practical advice. I did offer to call someone and put in a good word for him, but that's about it. What helped him most was just knowing that I had been through it. He must have looked at me and thought, *Hey, if this guy can get through what he just went through, I can surely get through this.*"

It's true that when we see another man who has just climbed out of a roller coaster—and he appears to have come through it okay—we are encouraged. If the guy came through with stronger faith or a better understanding of life, that's even better. That gives the rest of us courage to face our ups and downs.

Whether we like it or not, we are on this roller-coaster ride. The only thing we can choose is our attitude and how we act on the ride. Are we going to resist it the whole way, in stark terror, when we realize it's our time to take a plunge? Or are we going to remember someone else who has already been on the ride and came off smiling? If we remember someone who made it, we can throw up our hands and enjoy the ride (a little bit, anyway). Sure, everybody screams along the way—but imagine how much more stressful the experience would be if you never knew anyone who had been on a roller coaster before you and yet came back alive.

In one sense, that's the role I hope this book plays. I have put in a lot of time on roller coasters in the past few years, and I actually think I'm smiling more these days than I did in my pre-amputee days. One of the big reasons is that I know far more about who I am today than I did when I was still pitching for the San Francisco Giants. I am lighter by one limb than I used to be, but what God has given me far outweighs what I have lost.

I finally know who I am, and I am learning what I'm worth. These last few years have taught me so much about both of those areas that I can almost say I'm a new man. Life is far different now than it used to be—and it's far better. How so? I'm glad you asked. What God has been teaching me about the worth of a man is much too good to keep to myself.

Part Two

What I found

• • • • •

Chapter Seven

Two Great Discoveries

In professional athletics, people do not love you for who you are; all they care about is performance. I'm not whining about that, it's simply a fact.

I remember one time Jim Palmer and I were talking before a ball game, and he said to me, "People are going to remember you by your last appearance. You are only as good as your last pitch."

He was right. When I pitched well, good things were written about me in the papers; when I didn't, I was a bum. When I won, everybody loved me and put me on a pedestal. When I lost, they booed me and substituted a rail for the pedestal. In baseball, you are only as good as your last pitch!

You know, if that was the full extent of my worth as a man, I would be in deep, deep trouble. You know why? My last pitch in the major leagues didn't even make it to home plate!

What Is a Man Worth?

A few months after I lost my left arm and shoulder, I had to face some difficult questions. All my life I had trained and practiced and sacrificed and sweat to become a major league ballplayer, and I had made it. Then, at the height of my career, cancer took it all away from me. Life forced me to ask gut-level questions such as these:

- Who am I?
- What will I do now?
- Without my pitching arm, what am I worth?
- If my worth doesn't come from baseball, where does it come from?

I knew that a left-handed pitcher without a left hand wasn't "worth" anything to a major league ball club—not as a pitcher, anyway, and that's all I ever wanted to be. So now I had to answer a huge question to which I had previously never given much thought: What is Dave Dravecky worth, not as a baseball player, but as a man? And where does that worth come from?

I still wrestle with these questions, but I think I am a lot closer today to finding some satisfying answers than I was in 1991 right after the amputation. While I don't claim to be a theologian or a great Bible scholar, I am convinced that the Scriptures paint a remarkable picture of what a Christian man is worth. It's a worth that doesn't change with circumstances or vocation, doesn't depend on what we can or cannot do, and remains constant regardless of how our life situation may change. I assure you, this has been an incredible discovery for a man who formerly calculated his worth by the speed and accuracy of his fastball!

The Key: What God Has Done

So what is a man worth, especially a Christian man? What is he worth when everything about him is stripped away except for his very self? What is a man worth apart from his relationships or his ability to work and create? When a man stands naked before God, with nothing in his hands and no one at his side, what is he worth?

I am discovering that our worth as men is far beyond measurement *solely because of what God has done for us and in us.* Our worth stems not from what we have or what we do or what we control or whom we know, but from what God has done for us and in us. That was great news to me, because I always felt (regardless of what I said) that my worth stemmed from my performance—if I performed well, I was worth a lot; if I messed up, I wasn't worth much. But when I finally started to discover that my worth wasn't tied even a little to my abilities or my performance, but rather depended entirely and forever in what God already had done in and for me, my world suddenly opened up. I was free!

Of course, I am not the only one to make this tremendous discovery. Charlie Weidemeyer was an athlete and high school football coach when he came down with Lou Gehrig's disease. He went from being very active in his community to being barely able to breathe, speak, or even eat without help. Because he has lost all use of his voluntary muscles, he now spends most of his time in a wheelchair or in bed. When he realized his severe limitations and how much he would have to rely on Lucy, his wife, to take care of his basic needs, he said, "I just want to die."

When Lucy heard that, she declared emphatically, "Charlie, I'd rather have you as you are than not at all!"[1]

You see, Lucy understands (and feels!) that Charlie's worth is not tied up in what he can do, but in who he is as a man. That says a great deal because Charlie no longer amounts to very much in the eyes of the world. The day he expressed his wish to die, he was sincerely wondering if he had any worth at all. His wife inspired in him the will to live by convincing him that his worth was not found in what he could do, nor was it lost when he couldn't do much of anything. She found his worth in the man himself, the man inside the disabled body, the man she loved.

Lucy doesn't care if Charlie is still a coach. All that matters to her is that she can enjoy a relationship with him and share the love they have for each other. Charlie has incalculable worth regardless of his physical limitations.

This discovery marked a turning point in Charlie's life, and he has since gone on to inspire countless others. Charlie and Lucy travel the country, speaking to groups of youth and adults.

They encourage their audiences that each person has great worth, regardless of his or her limitations.

So Tell Me Another Story

I'd be willing to bet that some of you may be saying at this point, "Yeah, Bud, that sounds good—but is it really true?" That's a good question. How do we know that our worth as men does not depend on what we are able to do, but on what God has done in us and for us? How do we know that when we say things like this, we are not just whistling in the dark, trying to put a happy face on a bad situation? How do we know that a man's worth does not come from what he is able to do—his performance—but rather on whom God has made him to be?

When you want to know the truth, it's always best to go to the author of truth. I believe that God, in the Bible, gives us some phenomenally encouraging answers to these questions—answers that can literally change the way we operate and think about ourselves. I know that is what has happened for me. It has taken awhile, but I'm getting to where I need to be.

Perhaps you have already made these discoveries—they are nothing new to you. I wish I had made them long ago. But if you are still struggling with what you are "worth" as a man, maybe I can help point you in the right direction. I am convinced that the Bible gives us at least two big reasons for believing that our worth as men is immeasurable, not because of what we can do or accomplish, but because of what God has already done in us. Believe me, this is good news!

Two Big Reasons

When we lose an arm, mess up a relationship, get fired from a good job, or become bedridden through illness or accident, it is easy to get down on ourselves and start believing we are worthless. Yet the Bible tells us we have been made in the image of God—something that not even the angels can claim.

Genesis 1:26 states simply, "Then God said, 'Let us make man in our image, in our likeness, and let them rule over the fish of the sea and the birds of the air, over the livestock, over all the

earth, and over all the creatures that move along the ground.'"
If you look carefully through that first chapter of the Bible, you
will see that every other creature was created "according to its
kind"—but not human beings. They were made after the "image
of God."

I will be the first to admit that I don't know everything that
this little phrase is supposed to mean. I probably don't even
know most of what it means. But I do know this: If you are made
"in the image of God," you are top-of-the-line merchandise.
There is no higher "image" that you can be patterned after. You
may be inspired by the mountains, thrilled by the stars,
intrigued by the oceans, or mesmerized by this planet's wild
variety of plants and animals, but none of them can come close
to the wonder that is *us*. We are made in the very image of God!
I am, and so are you.

"But," someone will say, "isn't it true that Adam and Eve 'fell'
in the Garden of Eden through disobedience?" Yes, that is true.
They sinned and dragged all of their descendants (including us)
with them. But they were not "unmade" in God's image because
of their sin. The image was marred, but not destroyed or
removed. To this day, all men and women are born into the world
with God's image intact. That's why, for instance, James tells us
we should not cuss out those who irritate us—they are made in
God's image (James 3:9). They may not act like it, they may not
even know it, but the likeness is still there: They have been made
in the image of God and are therefore worthy of great respect.

(Although this is true, it's a sure bet you would not come to
understand this by hanging around a typical major league dugout
or clubhouse. In the heat of a game there aren't many ballplayers
or managers who will remind you—especially after you mess
up—that you were made in God's image. They are much more
likely to suggest a completely different heritage for you.)

Being made in the image of God gives us great worth—but
if we stop at this understanding, we will miss God's greatest
reason for believing in our worth. If you are a Christian—if you
have placed your faith in Jesus Christ as your Lord and

Savior—you have been redeemed from all the eternal conse-quences of the Fall. You are being "remade" into the image of Christ—spotless, pure, perfect, holy, righteous, and good.[2]

When we submit our lives to God by faith, he makes us into new creatures patterned after the image of his own dearly loved Son. This image has not been marred, damaged, or misshapen in any way; it is perfect. Therefore, as Christians we now have incredible worth. It does not vary with how we feel or change with what we do or don't do. Why not? Because it is "Christ in you, the hope of glory" (Colossians 1:27), and in Christ "are hid-den all the treasures of wisdom and knowledge" (Colossians 2:3), and "in this world we are like him" (1 John 4:17). We are heirs of God and co-heirs with Christ (Romans 8:17), and one day we will be conformed completely to his image (1 Corinthi-ans 15:49).

Guys, that is where our true worth comes from. Our worth is not based on our performance or our ability to perform; rather, it is found in the new person God has made us to be—a person of amazing worth.

The Difference It Makes

Realizing our worth and where it comes from makes a huge difference in how we live and relate to others. When we know how much we are worth because of what God did in us and for us, we realize we don't have to perform any longer to achieve "worth." Oh, people may still place unreasonable demands on us and dismiss us as worthless if we don't measure up to their expectations, but if we know our true worth and how God sees us, we are better able to cope and even thrive.

But let me make a qualification. I know something about qualifications, because most pro contracts have a few. Qualifi-cations are designed to clear up misunderstandings before they happen. I think one is needed here: *Knowledge* of our true worth does not make us invulnerable to *feelings* of worthlessness. Damaged relationships or the loss of a job or a serious health setback will continue to hurt. But knowledge of our true worth—especially when it's understood at the heart level and is embraced and celebrated—most definitely *does* soften the blows. As we grow closer to God and understand more and more fully who we are in Christ, a strange thing often happens: Our feelings deepen even while their ability to permanently damage or injure us grows less and less.

In the next few chapters I want to talk more about how work and human relationships affect our sense of worth as men. But for right now I want to concentrate on the central issue: our ongoing relationship with God.

Finding Ultimate Fulfillment

I have found that in order for me to find ultimate fulfillment and really *feel* the worth that God has built into me, my soul must rest in God. Every activity and every relationship on earth will fulfill its ultimate purpose only when it drives me toward a vital, growing relationship with him.

Developing good relationships is important, but those relationships are not the ultimate in life. Our relationships are good and necessary—they can warm our hearts and protect us from harm—but the ultimate purpose of every relationship should do two things: point us back to God and help us learn to love.

My family relationships are the most important things I have on earth. I love Jan, Tiffany and Jonathan, my mom and dad, my brothers and their families—but living out the love I feel is still a challenge for me. The challenge drives me back to God. I want to be the kind of man my family needs me to be. I want to honor my parents, and I want to love Jan as Christ loves the church. I want to be a good example to my children and not exasperate them by being too harsh. Yet the sheer desire to be that kind of man isn't enough to make it happen. I don't have the power to live up to my own right desires. That drives me to my knees, and that's good.

Promise Keepers is a great organization that draws men together, teaches them to build relationships with other men, and encourages them to promise to be faithful husbands, dads, Christians, and friends. A PK conference is a powerful and moving experience. To meet in a stadium with tens of thousands of other men—all seeking to do the right thing, all worshiping God together and pledging brotherly love—does something to you that is hard to describe. It's definitely an emotional high. When I attended one, I came away stoked, emotionally charged, and ready to get into a group where the guys committed themselves to hold each other accountable to keep their promises.

Relationships with other men are good and necessary— but if a guy goes to Promise Keepers and thinks, *All I need is this list of promises, a firm commitment, and the help of other guys to keep these promises,* he's in for a rude awakening. As long as Promise Keepers or any other program continually points a man back to reliance on God, it will fulfill its ultimate purpose. But if our participation in any organization or our relationships with other men cause us to depend on human willpower alone, they will fail us.

After I came down from the emotional high I enjoyed at the PK conference, I realized the true value of my relationship with the other men who shared my commitment. We could encourage each other not to give up when we fell short of our clearly defined promises. If I dared, I could go to the guys in my group and say, "Hey, guys, I'm falling short here. I need God's forgiveness for not keeping these promises. I need his power to keep them."

It is *God* who gives us the power to do what we cannot do on our own (or even with our brothers' help). I can keep the good promises I made only by staying close to God. The relationships I have with other men are helpful to the degree that they continually point me back to God. In other words, the ultimate purpose of all our activities and relationships is to drive us back to God. He is the source of all power, the source of all love, and the source of our true worth.

By the Checklist or From the Heart?

One day I was talking with my friend and former teammate Bob Knepper about how easy it is to make a checklist of what we are supposed to do and then to focus on the items on that list. We even measure our "worth" as Christians that way. Bob replied, "My relationship with God went from seeking a close relationship with him to 'read, study, learn the rules, and obey.' Instead of wanting to be intimate with God, I wanted to understand how to act and then to go out and do those things."

How quickly performance can rear its head! Even in our relationship with God.

Part of the reason for that is that it's harder for me to develop intimacy with God than it is to perform. Things have to be tangible in order for me to sense that I'm doing something truly worthwhile. I like to do things that move me closer toward a goal. But a goal like intimacy with God is not as tangible as I would like. So I tend to think, *If I do all these things, then it's working.* Our lives are measured by performance every step of the way, so when it comes to aiming for a close relationship with God, it's easier to veer toward checking things off a list than it is to actually get closer to God. But checklists will not enable us to get close to him, nor will they help us sense the worth that God has built into us.

I think a lot of Christian men have a tendency to make a list of the characteristics of a godly man—integrity, fidelity, honesty, kindness, compassion, diligence, and so on—and then try by sheer effort to produce those characteristics. We may find a man we respect, who lives a life of integrity, and try to live like him by doing what he is doing, instead of by developing the kind of relationship with God that that man has.

Jan and I have a dear friend named Leslie Andrews, who lost her husband, Jim, to cancer. Leslie told us how her brother, Jeff, always put her husband on a pedestal. He looked up to Jim and said to him many times over the years, "I try so hard to be like you." They had very different personalities, but Jeff kept saying, "When I think of what I want to be, I want to be like you—but I can't quite pull it off."

Just hours after Jim died, a letter from Jeff arrived at the house. That letter read, "Jim, I finally understand; I've tried to be like you for so long, and I've finally realized that you weren't acting. The things you did came out of your relationship with Jesus Christ. It wasn't that you got up every day and said, 'Okay,

I'm going to be really nice to Leslie today. I'm going to be really nice to my kids today; I'm not going to yell.' I finally get it. That is who you are because Jesus Christ is your Lord."

Jeff finally got it. He finally realized that he couldn't be a godly man merely by trying to imitate all the things he saw another godly man do. It wasn't Jim doing all those things anyway. It was Christ living in Jim and Jim responding to the Holy Spirit out of the love he had for God.

So what's the main lesson all of us can learn from Jim? Stay close to Jesus! Then, when we simply act like ourselves, we will reflect Jesus' love to the world. We won't even have to worry about a checklist, because we will be keeping it without trying.

May I ask you a personal question? Where is your heart in response to Christ? That is the central issue. If you have a relationship with God and are walking hand in hand with him, then the things on "the list" will be produced naturally in your life, like fruit on a tree. You can never gain God's approval by checking off items on a list. Remember, you already *have* his approval; now you simply need to live out of the freedom of the relationship you've been given.

And how do you do that? I'm convinced the right way is to remind ourselves often of how much God loves us—regardless of our abilities or disabilities, talents or deficits, riches or poverty. His love for us is changeless. And it is that love, remember, that gives us our unchanging worth.

The Love of God

My friend Chris Bingaman tells a true story from his life that brought home the love of God to me. In February of 1992, at the age of thirty-four, Chris was diagnosed with multiple myeloma, a cancer of the bone marrow. He has since received a bone marrow transplant and is free of all cancer cells. I will let Chris tell you the story in his own words.

> Prior to my diagnosis I frequently, throughout the day, had stabbing pains in my back and rib cage. This pain was so severe that I had to lay on the floor, try to prop up my

head on a pillow, and get my legs in a particular position to find some small measure of relief. At this time we didn't know what caused the pain; we later learned it was caused by a collapsed vertebrae in my back that was pinching the spinal cord.

The Saturday morning prior to my diagnosis, I was in our kitchen preparing breakfast when one of these bouts with pain struck again. Immediately, I went to our family room and fell to the floor, trying desperately to get some relief. While on the floor I heard a car pull up outside. I knew it was my dad, since he always stopped by to see how I was doing at this time of the morning.

My dad and I are very close. We are not only father and son, but he is also my employer. We work closely together in our family lumber business. We also hunt and fish together and cherish each other's companionship.

That Saturday morning, as I heard the door to our family room open, not a word was spoken. All I heard were Dad's footsteps coming toward me; I was in too much pain even to look up.

Dad had seen me in this position many times before, and he knew I was in severe pain. I felt his hand grab my shoulder. Then I began to feel his warm tears hit me on the cheek. Next, I heard my dad cry out to God, "O Lord, I pray that you would take this pain away from my son." As he continued to weep, he then cried out, "O God, give me his pain! I would gladly take his pain if I could."

I always knew my dad loved me, but at that moment I felt a greater love from my father than anything I had ever sensed before. My father would have given anything in the world to take away my suffering, but there was nothing he could do. While I later reflected on my father's love shown at my moment of greatest suffering, a thought hit me that relates to God's love for us.

My thoughts were drawn to another Father whose Son cried out to him just before his moment of greatest suffering. That Son was about to go through far more pain and suffering than Chris Bingaman ever knew. Jesus and his Father both knew what he was facing. Three times Jesus cried out to his Father to take away the cup of suffering he was about to drink by going to the cross. He cried out in agony, sweating great drops of blood. "Father," he said, "everything is possible for you. Take this cup from me. Yet not what I will, but what you will." Jesus knew that his Father had the power to take away his pain and prevent his suffering on the cross.

His Father, who surely loves Jesus far more than my earthly father loves me, chose not to take away his Son's cup of suffering. Why not? Because that was the price for our salvation.

I cannot fully comprehend that kind of love. But I accept it! I will never forget my dad's prayer that day or his warm tears on my cheek and the love I felt from him. That incident has given me a small glimpse of God's love for us.

I like the fact that God didn't approach us through religion but through the real life drama of a father and his son. Jesus, the God-man, came to earth as a man so we could relate to God on a man-to-man basis. God loved us so much that he gave his only Son to suffer and die as payment for our sins. I cannot fully understand that love any more than Chris could. But I, too, accept it. I wonder . . . do you?

Receiving the Father's Love

Men do not like to receive. We like to earn. We like to give. We like to pay for everything we get. Unfortunately, that attitude can get in the way of receiving the Father's love.

Jesus tried to give a true picture of our heavenly Father by telling a story of a father and his two sons (see Luke 15:11–32). They both had to learn the same lesson: how to receive their father's freely offered love.

The younger son in Jesus' story was rebellious. He lived in the lap of luxury while growing up. When he came of age, he took his inheritance and hit the road. He spent everything his father had given him on the very things that broke his father's heart. When he was out of money and his "friends" had abandoned him, he found himself living in a pigsty. When he finally admitted his pitiful situation, he decided to go home. He hoped he could come crawling back to his dad and at least get decent meals working as a servant. He rehearsed his speech all the way home, ashamed about his behavior and no doubt nervous about how he might be received.

When he was still a long way off, his father ran to him and embraced him—an action that no doubt surprised Jesus' listeners. The father hugged his son and kissed him and wouldn't even let him finish his prepared speech. Instead, he told his servants to throw a party. He put a robe on his son's shoulders, placed the family signet ring on his hand, and fully reinstated him to his place in the home. All the young man had to do was receive the love that his father so freely offered. This son had never done anything but disappoint his dad, yet that couldn't stop his father's love.

The older brother had a different problem; he was performance-oriented. He had spent his whole life trying to earn his father's love. That is why he grew baffled, jealous, and angry at his father's surprising behavior. "But Dad," he objected, "I stayed here, worked the land, and brought in the crops. I performed for you my whole life—but you never gave me a party like this!" His father tried to explain that all either of his sons had to do was receive what had always been there for them. The older son missed the father's love because he was too busy ticking off on his checklist the things he thought he had to do to earn it. When he saw his father freely giving his love to his rebellious brother, he became confused.

We can be like either of these sons. We may stay away from the heavenly Father because we are ashamed of how we have disappointed him. We may feel that we have broken every commandment God ever etched in stone. Or we may keep our distance because it ticks us off that God won't give his love to us in payment for our hard work. Both of the brothers in Jesus' story had to humble themselves if they were to receive the father's love . . . and so must we.

God wants all men, those who perform well and those who may not, to know that his love is a gift; it is free. There is nothing we can do to earn it, and there is nothing we can do that will disappoint our Father in heaven so much that he will withhold it.

God's love is there for the taking. But it must be as freely received as it is freely offered. That's the only way. And I'm glad it is!

What Are *You* Worth?

When I see how much value society places on performance, I realize how important it is to understand that our worth comes from who we *are*, not from what we *do*. The fact is, you are a man, made in the image of God. You are a man for whom Christ gave up his very life. And if you have accepted Christ into your heart, God is even now making you into the spitting image of Jesus himself.

Guys, that's a lot of worth! And it never changes—*never*. No matter what you do or don't do. No matter whom you know or don't know. No matter how much you have or don't have.

So does this mean our jobs and our relationships have no bearing on our sense of worth? I don't think so. At least, I know it wasn't in my own case. Before I lost my arm, I insisted that my identity and my worth were wrapped up in Jesus and not at all in my professional baseball career. But when I became an amputee and realized I would never throw another pitch, you better believe my sense of worth took a beating.

The question is, *Why?* If our worth as Christian men never changes, then why do major reversals in employment or relationships have such power to throw us gasping and moaning to the ground? When I lost my arm to cancer and with it my place in the major leagues, why did I end up feeling so utterly worthless? If my true worth is found solely in Jesus, then why did I *feel* so insignificant?

That is a crucial question, one that I want to look into in the next few chapters.

Notes

1. Charlie and Lucy tell their story in *Charlie's Victory: An Autobiography* (Grand Rapids: Zondervan, 1993).

2. See such passages as 2 Corinthians 3:18; Colossians 3:10; see also Romans 8:15–17; 2 Corinthians 5:17, 21.

Chapter Eight

Does Work Equal Worth?

Baseball fans should remember J. R. Richards, a feared pitcher for the Houston Astros from 1971 to 1980. When I was in the minor leagues, I once sat behind home plate and watched this mountain of a man pitch a 98 mph fastball and a 92 mph slider. He was a great pitcher until July 30, 1980. That was the day he suffered a career-ending stroke.

Since that awful day, James Rodney Richards has lost everything. Before his stroke, this six-foot eight-inch, 240-pound righthander was one of baseball's most dominating pitchers and commanded one of the highest salaries in the game at that time, earning some $850,000 a year. How good was he? "If I hadn't gotten sick, I could have broken all of Nolan Ryan's records," he said. That's quite a boast, but I think he might have done it. He was that good.

After a lengthy recovery, two broken marriages, and a string of bad investments, J. R. lost $300,000 in what turned out to be a bogus oil venture in California. His divorce from his wife, with whom he has five children, cost him $669,000. "I'm batting a flat zero in my life with investments," he said. "All it takes, regardless of how much money you make, is four or five sets of

101

people hitting you for a million or so a pop, and poof, it's gone!"
J. R. trusted agents, investors, and countless others, but none
of them cared about the man. They cared only about what he
could do, and when he couldn't do it anymore, they took advantage of him.

When his barbecue business failed and he lost his home in
a comfortable Houston subdivision, J. R. moved from friend to
friend for shelter. Ultimately, he was left on the streets. At least
twice in the past several months, for probably a week or so each
time, he lived under a freeway in southwest Houston. Virtually
no one recognized him—amazing, considering his size and once
immense popularity in Houston.

"I didn't want them to know who I was," J. R. said. "I am not
happy being under a bridge, but now I know what those people
go through. What I've tried to tell them and myself is that nothing lasts forever—only death. There aren't many people who
know how bad off I've been. Sometimes you just have to be a
man and trust God will help you out of this mess."

J. R. now works for an asphalt company that provides him
the use of a truck and an apartment, and friends told a newspa-
per reporter that there is no way to know how long the job or
apartment will last. On the day he was interviewed, he said he
had twenty dollars to his name.

When I hear stories like that, I think, *This guy was at the top
of his game, the top of the world; he had everything money could
buy.* But money and image both depend on performance, and
when J. R. could perform no longer, he was no longer needed.
Now he has to try to regain his sense of worth after losing everything.

I have no clue what it would be like to be in such a position,
but J. R.'s life mirrors the experience of so many who have made
it to the top but end up down and out. It happens. That's scary!
Our society evaluates worth on what you do and whether you
can do it better than the next guy.

I'm grateful I ended my career the way I did. Even though I
have certainly struggled, the fact is, I have a career. I have been

given something else to do. I have a dramatic story that is marketable. The way I left baseball catapulted me into another arena, which allowed me to maintain, for the most part, national exposure and many opportunities to remain visible. I am still asked to sign a lot of autographs—and when you get right down to brass tacks, all those things make me *feel* good. So, I probably *feel* more significant than J. R. Richards feels right now. And I am certain the world would say I am worth more than he is.

But am I really? Do my current activities make me worth more than his make him? The answer, of course, is an emphatic NO! While in the world's eyes you are only as good as your last pitch, in God's eyes your worth is found in whom he created you to be. Still, I'd be the first to admit that it doesn't always *feel* that way. I know Wayne McClure would agree with me.

What Can I Do?

Wayne McClure was a successful computer specialist and data processing manager for a major electronics manufacturing company. He was an early pioneer in the use of business computers and had been influential in applications development for a quarter of a century. Then diabetes took a terrible toll on his body. Wayne is now a double below-the-knee amputee. He's completely blind in one eye and has only partial sight in the other. Ten years ago, his physical limitations forced him into retirement.

A person Wayne didn't even know contacted our office a while back and asked me if I might give him a call to encourage him. I agreed, but I wasn't sure what to say. I mean, a double amputee—that's really tough. I've had my struggles, but his situation seemed far more drastic than anything I ever had to deal with.

When I finally called Wayne, he seemed like a pretty upbeat guy, but it was obvious he didn't feel as though he was worth a whole lot. He clearly didn't think of himself as significant and saw no meaning and purpose for his life. I tried to encourage him that God could bring something good out of the misfortune that had befallen him. I tried to convince him that he was needed—though I don't think he bought it.

"What can I do?" he protested. "I'm a diabetic. I've got no legs, and I can't see. What good can I do?"

I didn't have a fast answer.

I invited Wayne to meet me at church. He agreed to come, although he hadn't attended for some time. You see, with his two bulky leg prostheses, the time and effort required to change from his specially-fitted casual pants and shoes to appropriate church clothing just didn't seem worth it. He did show up to meet me though. The first day I saw him, I couldn't help but think, *This man does have something to offer.*

Our ministry, "Dave Dravecky's Outreach of Hope," focuses on encouraging cancer patients, amputees, and their families. I figured that if anybody could understand the pains and struggles of an amputee, Wayne could. So I asked him if he would like to be a volunteer.

At first he objected, "I don't know what I can do. I can't really see, I can't write. There are so many basic things that I just can't do."

"Well, you think about it and call me back," I replied. "I want you to be a part of what we're doing. I believe you have something to offer."

A couple of days later Wayne called me and said, "Okay. I'll come and give it a try."

Ninety percent of our mail comes from children, and it's impossible for me to respond to every letter personally. So we asked Wayne to reply to the kids who wrote to us. This man—who felt insignificant, worthless, of no value—suddenly found himself with an opportunity to encourage kids battling cancer and struggling with life after an amputation. Wayne could understand the enormous threats to health and self-esteem that these kids have to face. Because of what he had been through himself, he bubbled over with compassion for these kids.

Wayne came into the office that first day with a Sherlock Holmes magnifying glass so he could read the kids' letters. Soon afterward he had positioned an enlarging glass over the computer so he could see what he was writing. A little later he found software to blow up letters on the screen, big enough even for him to read. Now Wayne can sit down at the keyboard and see well enough to type his replies.

Since Wayne has joined our team, we have been getting more mail from kids than ever. But now, many of the letters aren't addressed to me; the kids want to talk to Wayne. This guy has his own fan club and he deserves it.

There is no way to measure the significance Wayne feels today. He has found something he can do that is worthwhile and appreciated. The positive contribution he has made in our office cannot be calculated; it is priceless. The world may be blind to Wayne's worth, but we are not. This guy is a stud in our office.

Does Job Equal Worth?

But this situation brings up a crucial question. Did we *give* Wayne his worth by offering him a job? Did his new work bestow on him worth that he didn't have before he joined us? Those are important questions, because a lot of us struggle in this very area.

In my own case, before the amputation I could stand in the clubhouse with Atlee Hammaker and swear up and down that my worth came from my relationship with Jesus Christ, not from my association with professional baseball. Yet after I lost my arm and could no longer play ball, I went through a huge battle with depression that centered on my worth as a man.

The question is, Why did I struggle like this? If I was right all along that my worth does indeed come from my relationship to Jesus Christ and not from the kind of work I do, then why, when baseball was taken away from me, did I often feel so worthless?

I don't think I'm alone here; I think a lot of men struggle with their worth when something goes haywire with a desirable job. Why should that be? If our worth as men doesn't come from our work, then why should we *feel* so worthless when our job situation takes a nosedive? And is this feeling right or wrong?

Wow! Those are pretty deep questions for a one-armed former baseball player, aren't they? But I think they are significant—so crucial, in fact, that I would like to take a little time to explore them. While we may not come up with the final answers, I do think we can grab some insights that can give us real help.

Sense of Worth Versus True Worth

It is incredibly easy for us to confuse our true worth with our *sense* of that worth. While the Bible teaches us that our true worth never varies, since it is based on God and not on us, yet our *sense* or *feeling* of that worth can vary tremendously. Often we do not "feel" that we have anything close to the worth that the Bible tells us is ours—especially when we lose a desirable job or become unable to provide for our family as we once did. Losing a great job can cause us men a lot of emotional pain and, as Wayne's story demonstrates, may also prompt us to live on a level far below what God intends for us.

It would be wonderful if our feelings always aligned with the truth, but we all know that's not the way it is. When we suffer a major job reversal, most of us take it personally. Not only do we get discouraged, we tend to think of it as an attack on our worth as men.

So what should we do? Try to ignore these feelings? That doesn't work either. I don't think we should ignore our feelings as much as try to align them with the truth. Our feelings are not unimportant and should not merely be disregarded—we were made to have emotions in the same way that God has emotions—but neither should we allow our fallen emotions to lead us in directions contrary to truth.

We men were made to work, so having a job does help us *feel* the worth God gave us when he made us in his own image. Wayne was not worth more after he began volunteering than before, but he sure *felt* his worth more. He finally discovered that what God said about him *felt* true. It's something like the line in an old song by the group America: "Oz never did give nothin' to the tin man / that he didn't, didn't already have." Wayne didn't add to his worth when he began volunteering at our ministry, but in a sense he did discover it. His worth was there all along, but it took a productive job to help him "feel" it.

Today, Wayne has no doubt that his life is worthwhile, even though he isn't paid a penny. The ability to earn a dollar never has been a good way to measure the worth of a man. That worth isn't found in material things that can be bought at the shopping mall. Wayne finally found meaning and purpose by giving of himself. By daring to find a new purpose in life, Wayne inspires all of us "has-been's" to become "could-be's."

In my own case, it was good to find some meaningful task to perform that helped me sense my worth. While I was going through my identity crisis, I needed a tangible boost. It was hard to deal with a body that wasn't whole anymore. I was deeply disturbed by what I saw in the mirror and consoled myself with how well I could perform in my new field of work. That was helpful for a while—yet I knew even then that there was more to me and the fullness of my life than my work.

Not being able to perform also helped me. When I couldn't perform as a baseball player anymore, I discovered my worth apart from having to perform. God, my family, and my friends loved me every bit as much when I couldn't play ball as they did when I could. I realized that not being able to perform as a ballplayer didn't make me worthless.

So why does work help us to "feel" our true worth? I believe that God has designed us in such a way that we sense our worth primarily through *productive activity* and through *relationships*. Neither work nor relationships give us worth in and of themselves, but they do help us to *sense* our true worth. Why? Because they reflect two important aspects of the image of God built into us.

Take work, for example. God himself is amazingly creative. He has never been and never will be a couch potato. In the beginning God created the heavens and the earth out of nothing. One big aspect of our being created in his image is the capacity and desire for productive activity. It is no accident that long before the Fall, God gave Adam a job: "The LORD God took the man and put him in the Garden of Eden to work it and take care of it" (Genesis 2:15).

When we are holding down a job we love and are providing materially for our family, we are taking the place God designed for us originally. In one sense we are more fully "acting out" God's image and Christ's character, and therefore we "feel" more deeply the worth that already is ours. Men were made to work, and when we find ourselves out of a job or unable to work, we feel an emptiness and even a sense of worthlessness. This feeling, of course, does not reflect the truth about our real worth—but it is understandable.

I believe that productive activity—a desirable job—is a great thing. It was designed to help us sense something of the enormous worth God has built into us as his sons. Our task is to enjoy it fully *in the capacity for which it was designed*, and not to confuse it with or put it in the place of our true, ultimate worth as men made in the image of God.

Our worth is *not* in our work; it is in who we are. Yet defining who we are and what makes life truly worthwhile is tough to hold on to, especially when life throws us a curve and we can't do what we had always dreamed of doing.

An Important Process

God created men to work; that is part of who we are. Remember how God dealt with the first man, Adam. No sooner did Adam appear on the scene than God put him to work naming animals and tending the garden. God told him exactly what he wanted him to do.

Unfortunately, we don't often get those kinds of specific instructions. At least, I don't. When I lost my arm, God did not start giving me a specific job description, so I had to figure out myself what I should do next. Fortunately, I didn't have to figure it out alone. Jan and I believe in praying and asking for God's guidance. As I spent time with God in prayer and talked with friends, I began to get direction regarding my new career.

Some of the direction came through doors that slammed shut or providential circumstances that seemed to lead us. Even before I fell from the mound in Montreal, God was speaking to me through Bob Knepper. Just a few hours before I fell, Bob told me, "God is giving you a platform through baseball to share the gospel with those who are hurting."

Then I went through all of the cancer treatments, grew uncertain of life, and was around people who were suffering. While I was in the hospital, Jan and I were overwhelmed with gifts. Bunches of flowers and fruit were going to rot if we didn't give them away, so we started visiting the other rooms, making the rounds, and bearing gifts to other sufferers in the hospital. I didn't see it at the time, but God was already at work in our hearts, leading us.

For the sixteen months following my amputation, I struggled to figure out what kind of value I had, especially concerning work. I wondered what I was supposed to do. Then I remembered a visit I had with a little boy suffering from leukemia. My heart had gone out to the little guy. That experience led me to see that I could encourage children who were suffering with cancer or amputation. I began doing what was in my heart out of love and a genuine concern for others. Then the Giants hosted "Dave Dravecky Day" at Candlestick Park and wanted to give us a financial gift. That gift was the beginning of our ministry, a ministry that we never intended to start.

The whole time I was worrying about what I was supposed to do, I was on my way to doing it. God was using baseball as the platform for doing something special in our lives, just as Bob Knepper had predicted. God had plans for me all along—just as he does for you. I had to go through a process of seeking God to find my way. I had many choices about what direction to take. Jan and I had to be willing to seek God about the direction of our lives and to follow his leading. And the process didn't stop once we began the ministry. I continually seek God about what he might want me to do in the future.

Finding productive work is an important, God-given way for men to sense the tremendous worth already built into them. When we try to figure out why we are here and what we are supposed to be doing with our lives, it is vital that God be in the picture. He created us with a purpose. He knows who we are and what we can do. If we ask him to lead us, he will. It may be a long process, but he will lead. Normally, God leads us according to the growing desires of our heart. Most likely he will lead you in a direction in keeping with your heart. He wants whatever work you do to help you sense your worth as a man.

But as important as productive work is to sensing our true worth, "career" and "job" can lure us into a deadly trap. That's what I want to talk about next.

Chapter Nine

A Deadly Trap

Most men get a tremendous sense of worth out of what they do for a living. They quickly discover that the better they perform in the workplace, the more accolades come their way. As a result, it's easy to imagine that the better they perform, the more they are worth.

And in one way, that's exactly right. It's perfectly okay to say that a starting pitcher is "worth" more to his club than is the ballboy, or that a lead engineer with 2,345 patents to his name is "worth" more to his company than a part-time janitor who sleeps on the job.

Yet in another sense, that's not right at all. When I talk about *worth* in this book, I am talking about a man's true worth—his worth in God's eyes regardless of what he does or how much he makes. In that sense, how does our performance fit with our sense of worth? Whether the field is sports, business, or ministry, the questions and issues are the same.

Bob, a friend of mine who is active in several recreational sports leagues, admits he is performance-oriented in all areas of life: at work, in sports, in expecting his sons to perform with excellence. He once asked me a good question: "Dave, you used to measure yourself by how you performed on the baseball field. How do you measure yourself now? Is it still primarily by how you perform?"

As an athlete, the heartbeat of my professional life was to measure myself by performance. So when I had to change careers, I simply shifted from one kind of performance to another. When I left baseball and entered the field of publishing and public speaking, I still measured everything I did and constantly judged my performance. I measured myself by the response I received from the audience, by how well my books were selling, or by how well the media received me.

Is that all bad? I don't think so. But the challenge we face is to balance our desire to do a great job at whatever we do with a healthy understanding that our worth as men is not earned by achieving success. As I said in the previous chapter, it is true that business success makes us *feel* as if we are worth more, but it doesn't *actually* make us worth more. We should be thankful that God has enabled us to work and thereby to give us the ability to express part of his image. But if we start thinking that success gives us more worth or that failure takes away our worth, we will wind up with some big problems in a hurry.

The Desire for Excellence

As a matter of principle, I aim to do my best at whatever I do. The Bible is full of lessons about excellence. We are told to run in such a way to win the prize, to box as if it's a real fight, not as if we're just beating the air (1 Corinthians 9:24–27). Jesus said that everyone has been given various talents and that we will be held accountable for investing those talents wisely and giving God a good return on that investment (Matthew 25:14–30; Luke 12:42–48). The Scriptures also tell us that we are a part of the body of Christ and that each one of us has a responsibility to fulfill our duty to the rest of the body (Romans 12:3–8; Philippians 2:1–4).

All these illustrations say the same thing: Part of our calling is to perform. We are instructed to do whatever we do as if we were doing it for the Lord himself, because in reality we are (Colossians 3:17). We are even promised rewards according to the level of our performance (1 Corinthians 3:12–15; 2 Corinthians 5:9–10). These passages all tell me that there is nothing wrong with devoting ourselves to excellence and performing to the best of our abilities.

Yet we must continually remind ourselves that God has given us tremendous worth completely apart from how we perform. He never looks at what we do as a way for us to prove our worth. He wants our desire for excellence, our commitment to perform well, to flow out of the confidence that we *already have* worth in his eyes. He created us to do good works (Ephesians 2:10), but we do not have to do the good works to establish our worth. Our worth is fixed in God's eyes because he created us in his own image and because he sent his sinless Son to die for us.

We must never forget that God does not measure our performance by comparing us to the next person. He will measure our performance (at work, morally, in our relationships, in all of life) by looking at how well we did with the talents and opportunities he gave us. He will not merely look at the bottom line in terms of sales or wins or dollars earned. He will look at how we have treated the people we worked with while we labored to achieve our goals.

The drive to be successful is a powerful force in our culture, but when this drive prompts us to judge a man's worth by comparing him to others, it is both dangerous and deceptive. The very term "success" comes from a root word that means "to be a successor, one who rises up to take another's place." If a man measures his worth by comparing himself to other men and by trying to rise higher than the next guy, he will have to become self-centered to "succeed." And when "success" is the ultimate goal, a man will do whatever it takes, even if that means tearing down, undermining, or humiliating his competitor. The success-driven man makes himself feel more worthy by making others feel less worthy. He puts himself up by putting others down.

A man who judges his worth by his level of "success" will likely be so driven to perform at an excessive level that he will compromise his character, his morals, and his time with his family. The man driven to perform may excel in a career or in another isolated area of his life, but he is going to lose out somewhere, and so will those who make up part of his life.

Looking Out for Others

To be a real winner on the field of life, a man must look out not only for his own interests, but also for the interests of others. To be a good team player you cannot afford to think only of yourself. You have to choose to use your talents to cooperate with your teammates for the common good. Sometimes that means letting somebody else get the glory—if that's what it takes for the team to win, that's what you do. And you do it gladly.

I'd be a fool to think that I could have won a single baseball game by great pitching alone. I couldn't win on my own in baseball, and we can't win at life by trying to succeed on our own. Giving a great performance means we cooperate with others to achieve team success. Trying to promote and protect ourselves will never get the job done.

In every line of work, whether it's sports, ministry, or business, there are times when the pressure is on. There are times when somebody on the team drops the ball or misses a play. In those situations, the way we treat each other is what makes the difference between winning and losing; it certainly makes or breaks team morale. I think God cares about our performance toward each other in those kinds of situations just as much as (if not more than) he does about whether we make the play or close the deal.

I encourage you to look at those with whom you work in a fresh light. You can allow God to work through you to affirm the worth of your co-worker. That is far more valuable than merely the work you do!

So—Is He or Isn't He?

So now the $64,000 question: Am I still performance-oriented? Sure I am. I just make sure that, to the best of my ability, I perform in a way that does not tear others down. When we do our work with a view toward excellence, whatever that work is, we will be helped to gain a stronger sense of our worth as men.

Yet there is a common and deadly trap concerning work and worth that a lot of us fall into. Sometimes a job or an activity gives us such great fulfillment that it is easy to forget that, as good as it is, it only dimly reflects the true worth we have as new creatures made in the image of Christ. The feelings involved with a satisfying career can be so pleasurable and so affirming that we begin pouring all our energy into it. Before long we are not only getting our *sense* of worth from our job, but we have shifted to believing that our worth *itself* comes from our job. And that is a lethal error.

Productive activity was designed by God to remind us of the inheritance we will one day fully receive as his children. But when we mistake work for the real thing—and that work is taken away—we are left with a sense of tremendous failure and great worthlessness. Larry found that out the hard way.

Larry's Regrets

We all start out the same—hoping for the best and dreaming of what we want to do when we grow up, how we're going to make our mark on the world, what kind of family we want, what sort of home we'll buy, what we hope for our kids, and so on. We all make decisions about how we will use our time and opportunities. Yet what looks great from the starting blocks can look very different from the finish line.

Larry is a Christian who tried to set his priorities according to what he believed God wanted him to do. He makes sure his whole family is in church together every Sunday. For the past seventeen years Larry has worked hard to build his business, and until lately he's exceeded his hopes. He has a twenty-year marriage to a beautiful wife who is devoted to him, to their family, and to God. He has a son who is headed off for college and a daughter in tenth grade who is at the top of her class academically and socially. He has provided well enough for them to live in a spacious, hilltop home, complete with a swimming pool and basketball court. Most of his friends admire Larry, and people who know him only casually think he has the best that life has to offer.

But Larry is no longer so sure. Certain events have caused him to reflect back over his life, and he is not entirely pleased with what he sees.

For the past couple of years, Larry's company has been teetering on the brink of collapse. The firm has filed chapter eleven bankruptcy and has laid off most of its employees. The corporate officers who stayed, including Larry, have not taken a salary for over a year while working to save the business. Seventeen years of toil and trouble have come to less than nothing, and many of Larry's friends are telling him he should throw in the towel. But a guy like Larry doesn't throw in the towel as long as there is a shred of hope. He has invested his entire adult life in this company, and he can't easily walk away from it.

Related issues in Larry's life have given him pause, too. The reason Larry worked so hard in the first place was to provide a good life for his wife and kids. Then a couple of years ago Larry's son dropped a bombshell: His fifteen-year-old girlfriend was pregnant. Larry was going to be a grandfather before he turned forty. It was the last thing he expected from his son, who had always been involved in church and was a star athlete and an honor student. I think I'll let Larry himself tell you about his reflections.

> I work with a specialized construction company and we travel all over the country. I'm gone a lot, and the business is here in Sacramento. My wife and I made a commitment when we got into this business that I would stay down here during the week and she would take care of the kids in our hometown about a hundred and fifty miles away. So the natural tendency of things was for me to be gone a lot. In the process of being gone, my kids have grown up.
>
> The business has been in the dirt for a couple of years now, and you've heard the story about my son becoming a father during his junior year in high school. Last night, I guess the chickens really came home to roost when I

attended my son's high school graduation. As I watched him walk out onto that stage and sit down—then somebody handed me his daughter—I thought, *I have a grand-daughter and my son is graduating. Where did my life go?*

I thought about the past few years with the business. I have seen millions of dollars slip away. When the chips were down, I kept working full speed, even after I hadn't been paid for a year, and then the company took a $4,800.00 check that was owed to me. This is the company for which I totally sacrificed my family life. I put the company at the top of my list all these years, but it certainly didn't put me first. That was a wake-up call!

I thought, *All that time, all my sacrifices—it ain't been worth it! My son! My daughter! My wife! This is bogus! There ain't no dream here. I've been bought out by the almighty buck.*

It wasn't anything I set out to do. It was a transition over ten years of putting my head down and going for it. And in those ten years, my kids grew up.

I feel guilty because I haven't been home very much. I would have liked to have been there for their first steps or taken the kids to school on the first day. I never got to do the things that a regular dad did because I was out of town during the week. I never got to coach the team or anything like that. And when I had time with my son on the weekend, I was Donald Duck crazy; I mean, I wanted the kid to be the best at everything. I required it. It's a wonder that my son turned out as well as he did. He's on his way to college with a great future ahead of him, even if he has made some mistakes. He's a good kid, but I wonder how much my absence has hurt him.

My advice for somebody young who wants to get started on the right track is this: Keep your focus on what's really important. Time is so valuable and it really does slip away! Life is fragile, and you've got to handle the time in and around your family as precious. If you don't, it will get lost. And you can't start over again because the time is gone.

Someday you will have to ask yourself if time spent somewhere else was worth the price. When you do wake up and smell the coffee, there's no turning back. It's done. Then you have all kinds of questions to which you will never know the answers. *What if I had been there and not gone after the "almighty dollar" to get this company going and keep it afloat?* I'm left wondering because there is no way for me to know how things might have been if I had been home more.

You know the old saying that everybody has a price? It's true! We wanted to be financially set so that we could have quality time to spend with our family, but that's a lie from the pit! My wife and I said, "Hey, if this business is going to succeed, it will take sacrifice, and down the road we'll be able to afford to have some quality time together." But when we got down the road, we realized that some of the opportunity to have quality time with our kids was lost forever.

I feel cheated, and that angers me because I don't like to be cheated at anything. If I'm beat straight out, I'll take my lumps; but if somebody cheats me, it makes me want to fight. But whom do I fight? Do I fight myself? I mean, *I* made the decision. Ultimately it was on *my* shoulders.

When your heart and soul go into something you believe in and are committed to, and then the business goes under, you've given your precious time away—and for what? I sacrificed my life for this business and it ended up in the ditch. We still could turn it around, but even if we do, where does that leave me? I had to face the fact that I made some wrong decisions, even though the desire in my heart was to do what was right.

You know what? If I had it to do all over again, in 1984 when they offered me a piece of this business, I'd turn it down flat. I would have gone back to school, got my teaching credential, and probably taught high school where my kids attended. I would not have made the big money or had the big write-ups in this magazine or that, but I would have been available to my family.

I may have realized this a little late, but at least I can pass on what I've learned: It's not worth it to give the best of your life to a career that can't love you back.

Larry's younger brother, Bob, wanted to make sure that Larry understood his warning would not go unheeded. "Larry," he told him, "I don't want you to think that your mistakes have been wasted. You have a little brother [which is a funny statement coming from a guy who stands six foot, four inches tall] who has been watching every decision you've made. I have learned that it's not worth the big money to take a job that would take me away from my family. I don't say this to embarrass you. I just want you to know that your mistakes have not been worthless. They have proven extremely valuable to me and my family."

I wonder—is it possible that you need to learn from Larry too? Do you need to step back and see whether you are chasing a dream of quality time "down the road," only to miss out on important moments with your family *now*? Is what you are investing your life in really going to pay off? Bob is not the only one who can learn from his big brother's regrets; we all can. Career and work are important, but they are not everything. So let's not treat them as if they were.

The Baseballs on My Shelf

If you walked into my office, you would probably notice the baseballs on my shelf. Each one commemorates a special achievement from my baseball career. There's the ball from my first win as a professional ballplayer in the minor leagues, when I played in Shelby, North Carolina. There's the ball from my first major league win when I was playing for the San Diego Padres: July 4, 1982. I pitched against the San Francisco Giants and the guy I beat was Atlee Hammaker (who later became my close friend). When I put that ball on my shelf, I did not know that exactly five years later, on July 4, 1987, I would be traded to the San Francisco Giants. I also have my 1983 autographed All-Star ball and my 1989 "Earthquake World Series" ball autographed by all the guys on our team.

Each one of those baseballs on my shelf are prized, but there are two that I prize more highly than the rest. The first is the ball from my best pitching performance in the major leagues, when I threw a one-hit shutout against the Los Angeles Dodgers. The other is the ball that I hit out of the park for my first home run in the major leagues. Again we were playing against the Dodgers. We were at Jack Murphy Stadium in San Diego in 1986, the count was three and two, and I was batting off a left-handed pitcher named Dennis Powell. Those achievements are indelibly etched into my memory.

Just because I could no longer play the game, I didn't take the baseballs off my shelf. I prize the memories and the accomplishments they represent. Looking at them helps me to remember that I have enjoyed great accomplishments in my work life. We all feel better about ourselves when we consider our work achievements.

But you know what else encourages me? I didn't know what the future held when I pitched my first major league win against Atlee Hammaker. I had no way of knowing what a good friend Atlee would become to me. I had no way of knowing about the other balls that would one day be placed on my shelf alongside that first one.

I'm encouraged to know that there are shelves yet to be filled in my future, just as there are in yours. There are accomplishments waiting to be achieved and friendships waiting to be made. Maybe we should all put up an empty shelf, in faith that what we are dreaming of now will, one day, be achieved. God alone knows what could end up on our shelves!

But let's make sure that what winds up on the shelf is not us. God has made us to work, and productive activity helps us to sense the great worth he has given us. Work, however, is not everything. It's a trap and a lie to believe that work or career gives us our worth. Don't exchange the worth God has given you for some shiny trophy earned in the business world. It may look enticing now, but in the end, it will betray you. Too late you will discover that your very life was placed on the same shelf as a very tarnished, utterly worthless trophy.

So please, don't sit on the shelf. You are much too valuable for that.

Chapter Ten

Better Than All the Jewels in the World

I used to think I was basically a pretty good guy. I heard about God's grace, but I didn't feel as if I had to rely on that too much. As long as life was fair and things were going my way, I thought things were fine. But when life turned unfair, when I was hurting really bad, suddenly it was a different story. I saw just how ugly Dave Dravecky can be.

To this day I don't understand how my wife put up with me through that difficult time. I don't understand how someone could love me in the midst of all my anger, moodiness, selfishness, and all the other unpleasantness that came to the surface when I was hurting.

And yet she did. Through Jan, I knew God still loved me, even when I was hurting too bad to be good. There was a beauty about what God did in me. When I was in pain and the ugly side of me came out, I somehow knew—even in the midst of that—that God still loved me and that I had unbelievable worth in his eyes. This is hard to describe because it is beyond my full comprehension. I found God's grace most powerful in times of pain, when I knew his love even though I felt unlovable. All I could do was accept it; that changed me for the better.

My experience taught me something not only about God, but also about how our most cherished relationships help us to sense our God-given worth, regardless of the circumstances. Most of us, I think, come to appreciate our true worth primarily through work and through our relationship with our wives. When we find ourselves desperately struggling with who we are as men, most likely we are "under attack" in one of these two crucial areas. We have talked about the first area; now it's time to focus for a while on the second.

God and Relationships

Why do we sense so much of our worth as men through our relationship with our wives? I think the reason has to do with God's own intense involvement in relationships. Before the creation of the world, the three members of the Trinity enjoyed a perfect, loving relationship with each other. God was never "lonely," despite what you sometimes hear. He has always enjoyed phenomenal relationships. And he wanted that part of himself to be reflected in his creation.

When Adam was formed in God's image, a significant part of that image was his capacity and desire for relationship. I do not believe it is any accident that God said before creating Eve, "It is not good for the man to be alone. I will make a helper suitable for him" (Genesis 2:18).

An intimate husband-wife relationship is the closest thing we have to the intimate relationship that exists within the Trinity. When I grow close to my wife, I most fully "feel" the worth that God has built into me. Human beings were made for relationships, and when we find ourselves deprived of them or challenged in them, we feel an emptiness and even a sense of worthlessness. This feeling, of course, does not reflect the truth about ourselves, but it is certainly understandable.

When we struggle in our marriages, we can feel as though our worth as men is being challenged. Probably most of us tend to look at all our deficits, while our wives seem to evaluate us on a different basis. They understand that the worth of a man isn't calculated by adding up the good he has done and subtracting the bad. A godly wife knows that her husband's worth comes from who he is, not by what he does or doesn't do.

That's what I think, anyway. But who am I? So I decided to explore my conclusions by talking to a few women whose friendship Jan and I value. What worth did they see in their husbands? I learned some interesting things that may alter the next self-evaluation you do.

Worth More Than Jewels

Earlier I introduced you to Leslie Andrews, who lost her husband, Jim, to cancer. What was the worth of this man to his wife? I'll let her tell you in her own words.

> About eight years into our marriage, the Lord started doing some major work on me. It was a painful experience, and it was hard for Jim to go through that with me. But because of Jim's love, I was secure and I felt safe. I knew that no matter what I went through or who I became, Jim loved me and would continue to love me. I sit here saying that Jim did this for me, but Jim would never take the credit. I now realize that Jesus gave me Jim to love me and take me to the place God wanted me to go. I needed a flesh-and-blood Jesus in my life, and that was my husband.
>
> Jim approached the practical aspects of life by living responsibly so that he could live generously. He took care of us. He worked diligently so we would be secure financially instead of having to worry about money. I knew I was cared for, not just emotionally, but practically. He provided for me and protected me, so I could care for our children. That was incredibly important that he provided for us so well! But that isn't what we miss. We don't miss the dollars he brought home.
>
> I miss having somebody to help me share the responsibility. I don't like being the one who says, "The buck stops here," even though I can do it. What I miss is the camaraderie. I miss his companionship, I miss sharing my heart,

my life with him. When you've had a soul mate for sixteen years and suddenly he's not there . . . it's a huge loss.

He was a gentle and faithful man, a treasure. Even though our boys lost their father, they lost the treasure I married. I knew I married a saint. His integrity, his strength, and his character were obvious to everyone who knew him. He had a good sense of humor, even though it was dry. He was very much involved in life, even when he was dying. There was a lot of passion in Jim. He had great passion for life, for me, for the boys, and for the Lord. His greatest passion was for God. Because he was such an incredible man, our loss is deep, hard, and painful.

Jim wasn't just all these things that we're talking about. How can I say this? He was my husband. He was a man I dearly loved and gave myself to until death. I knew how very special he was; that's why I didn't want to lose him. Unfortunately, his death came much sooner than we ever anticipated. The major reason Jim didn't want to die was because he didn't want to leave us. He wanted to stay in this life to love us. I think he knew even better than I did how hard it was going to be for me to lose him. And yet, he encouraged me to live. He loved me, Dave. . . .

Leslie cried as she spoke of her husband. She spoke of her frustration at her inability to convey with mere words the worth of the man she loved. She continued:

I want you to understand. I was his pearl and he was mine. Actually, I was his pearl and he was my oyster. We did that for each other. We gave each other a safe place to let the grit grow into something beautiful. I don't know how to put the loss of that into words. How can you put a high enough value on that?

Dave, how do you say to a man who is reading your book, "Don't be afraid to let your wife develop into who God wants her to be. Don't be afraid of the process that she's going to have to go through to get there. Don't be afraid of some of her depression or anxiety or if she becomes diffi-cult to live with for a while. It's scary to watch someone you love go through that. It's painful for both of you. But if you support her, and hold her, and love her in the midst of that; if you're willing to let God do that through you in her life, you will end up with a jewel. And your value in her life will be worth more than all the jewels in the world."

As I sat there listening to Leslie's story, I wondered what would come next. I didn't have to wait long. Another friend who had heard the whole thing was ready to speak up.

Worth All the Pain

"Leslie," this woman said, "your husband sounds like a wonderful man. He lived his life without ever bringing shame on your family. And I can see why he and his love are worth so much to you. You have been blessed. But there is something I must say that may help some of the men out there who will read Dave's book—those who haven't lived their lives with the same kind of integrity Jim did.

"You see, my husband loves me, too. I was his pearl and he was my oyster. His love made a safe place for me to grow and become the woman God created me to be. He helped me overcome so many of my insecurities.

"Then several years ago he confessed to me that he had been involved in sexual sin. I was devastated, because I thought he was the perfect husband. He was a saint, but he was a saint who had to call on the grace of God for betraying my trust and breaking our marriage vows. We went through hell—at least it felt like all the forces of hell were ravaging us. We lost so much because of what he had done. We went through seven years of tremendous pain and insecurity in our relationship to mend the damage. But our marriage is better now than ever, and his worth has been reaffirmed in my eyes.

"There is something I want you to know, Dave," she said to me, "something the men reading your book *have* to know. I love my husband with all my heart. I value him as much as I hear Leslie trying to express how much she loved Jim and cherishes his memory and all he has done in her life."

Then she looked back at Leslie. "You were saying that it is not what Jim did that made you value him. You loved the man; the value you found in him was based in who he was and how he loved you. I feel the same way. It is not what my husband has done that is good that makes me love him; nor has what he has done that was bad made me not love him. Even though he compromised his commitment to me, he is still more valuable than words can express. What is the worth of this man and the love that we share? There is no adequate way for me to express what he is worth, except maybe to say that he is worth far more than the pain and hard work it took to hold our marriage together."

I didn't know what to say. This friend's response was totally unexpected, but I appreciated seeing both sides of the same kind of love. One of these women saw a man live out his days, always true to his convictions. The other saw her husband fail in one of the most painful ways a man can fail his wife.

But the message was the same. The worth of the man was not established by what he did, even though it was very good. The worth of the man was not destroyed by what he did, even though it was very bad. The worth of the man was found in who he was and the love he was willing to share with his wife.

Whoa! How many men look at themselves in that way? Yet what a difference it would make if they did!

Sharing Your Soul

One day I was talking with Bob Knepper about the worth of a man. We started our conversation out on the deck surrounding his beautiful home when a sudden thunderstorm drove us inside. In a few moments Bob's wife, Teri, joined us. I'm glad that she did, because it gave me a chance to ask her about Bob's worth to her.

We had been talking about how Bob had begun his relationship with Teri by sharing his heart and soul with her. He didn't become a Christian until after they were married, but he always wanted to be a good husband. He told us about how he changed over the years from merely sharing his heart with his wife, to trying to complete a checklist of what he thought it meant to be a Christian husband. One of the things he tried to be for her was "strong." Yet by trying to be strong, he stopped sharing everything that was going on with him, especially the part of his life where he felt a lack of strength. Then recently, Bob was working through some issues that caused him to let down and pour out his heart to Teri again, as he did after they first met.

I asked Teri, "Which is worth more to you, having Bob perform a list of activities characteristic of a good husband, or having him share his soul with you?" This is what she said:

> When I first met Bob, all through our short courtship, he bared his heart to me. He let me get to know him through letters that we wrote back and forth. In our first couple years of marriage, he bared his heart without reservation. That was what I loved because I knew him as I've never known anyone. To think that we had such a close relationship was just so wonderful to me. He told me his dreams, his hopes, his hurts. The times he was up and the times he was down—he shared them all with me.

One of the hopes Bob shared with his wife was his desire to become a rancher. He had always dreamed of owning a big spread. When he retired from baseball, he bought several acres in Oregon and settled down to what he thought would be his career for many years. The only problem was that his family didn't like ranching.

Bob could have insisted on staying with it—it was what he always dreamed of doing, after all—but Bob is a man who is committed to blessing his wife. He teaches marriage classes about the importance of considering a spouse's happiness whenever you make a decision. He wanted to do something enjoyable for his whole family, so he gave up his ranch even though he wasn't sure what his next career move would be. By being true to his love for his wife, he got some direction about what *not* to do. He's still unsure what he will end up doing long-term, but because he is seeking God's guidance and is motivated by love and faithfulness to his family, I know he will find his way to some kind of fulfilling work.

That kind of love says something to a wife. It demonstrates to her not only that her husband has great worth, but that he understands and appreciates her worth as well. Maybe that's why Teri looked straight into Bob's eyes and said, "I love you for who you *are*. When you share yourself with me, it makes me fall in love with you that much more. God never finishes our love. I keep thinking that I can't have more love for you, but God keeps bringing more love for you into my heart."

Wow! Listening to each woman talk about the worth of the man she married makes me think we should listen to our wives more closely. If we do, I think we will find that they peg our worth at levels far higher than we do ourselves.

A Commitment to Servanthood

As great as it is to understand something of the great worth God has built into us as men, it is not enough. We are called to "live out" that worth in those around us, especially our wives. A big part of that "living out" is a commitment to servanthood, the kind of servanthood Bob displayed when he gave up a cherished dream for the welfare of his family.

It's easy to get confused about our purpose in this world. Our culture tells us that the guy who dies with the most toys wins. It tells us that power and prestige, fame and fortune are what it's all about. But I've seen far too many men who had all those things and yet were desperately unfulfilled. Remember Larry?

Whatever a guy sees as his goal in life will determine what he commits himself to do. If you think you have to be rich financially to be fulfilled, you are going to commit yourself to a different set of priorities than the man who is committed to being the best husband he can be. That's just the way it goes. Jesus put it this way: "Where your treasure is, there your heart will be also" (Matthew 6:21).

I am committed to following Jesus Christ. That key commitment determines many other commitments in my life. One day when his disciples were bickering about who among them was the greatest, Jesus said, "If anyone wants to be first, he must be the very last, and the servant of all" (Mark 9:35). Many times he insisted that anyone who wanted to be great in God's kingdom had to become a servant. So if I commit myself to follow Jesus, that means I must also commit myself to servanthood—especially in marriage.

I have tried it both ways. I tried seeking fame and fortune, power and prestige. I found a measure of what I sought, but it never brought the complete fulfillment I hoped it would. Then I sought God through a relationship with Jesus Christ and asked him to help me be of service to others. I discovered that to be tremendously fulfilling.

While it's sometimes a struggle, I continue to want to serve others. As I do so, I keep finding a sense of fulfillment that I never found any other way. My commitment to service has helped me realize my worth as a man far more than living merely to serve myself. And in many ways, the greatest service I can perform is for my family—especially my wife. But such service doesn't come easily. To be honest, before the service comes something else: commitment.

Commitment to Marriage

The world has a funny definition of commitment; no doubt that is why there is such a high divorce rate. Our society puts so much emphasis on "love" and "attraction" that we lose sight of the necessity of commitment. The world defines commitment based on feelings: "I will stay committed to you as long as I have certain kinds of feelings for you." But when the feelings are gone, it's okay to move on in search of the next commitment where, it is hoped, the feelings will stay. In my experience, feelings come and go, even in the best of relationships. And if you are not committed, relationships will come and go too.

As a kid, I "loved" baseball. I was "attracted" to the prospect of being a major league ballplayer. But I understood that my love of the game was not enough to take me to the major leagues. Love of the game is what gave me the determination to make it to the major leagues; love of the game gave me my commitment. I had to work hard consistently to reach the majors, and then I had to work just as hard to stay there. There were plenty of times when it was painful, but I had to do it because I was committed.

The same holds true for marriage. My love for Jan is what gives me the determination to commit myself to her for life. Marriage is based on love, but it takes determination and consistent work to keep the relationship in good shape.

No one ever made it to the major leagues with half-hearted effort. And I don't believe a marriage can make it if either partner gives less than a whole-hearted commitment. I have heard people talk about marriage as if it were a 50/50 proposition, but giving 50 percent to your marriage is a half-hearted effort. That won't cut it; each partner has to give 100 percent for a marriage to work.

I know there are times when one partner gives 100 percent and the other person does not. The other person may even walk away when you are giving your all. I know people have lost marriages to which they were completely committed, and I don't know how to console them. But if you are in a marriage or considering marriage, you can prepare yourself to make it work by adjusting your level of commitment to 100 percent. Choose to give it all you've got.

A Tall Order

By this point, you may be wondering, *Dave, what does all this have to do with the worth of a man?* Just this: Once we begin to understand our enormous worth as men made in God's image, we are able to "live out" that image in the way we treat our wives. Our commitment to them should reflect God's unchanging commitment to us.

A tall order, you say? You bet. But I'm not in this alone, and neither are you. God has a vested interest in our success, and with infinite resources at his disposal, we can get the job done. That is, as long as we are willing.

The question is, are we?

Chapter Eleven

No Stats on Being a Good Dad

One of the great things about baseball is that everything is measurable. There are three outs to an inning and nine innings to every game. Performance is clearly measured by the statistics. I knew when I was doing great, where I needed to improve, and how I compared to every other pitcher who ever played the game. Since my stats were pretty good, I took comfort in them.

When it comes to being a dad, however, there ain't no statistics at all! The only "statistic" is whether your child survives and becomes a decent human being.

Many guys struggle with this. We want to be able to measure our worth in tangible ways; we like knowing for a fact that our lives amount to something. Whether that's dollars earned, sales closed, people helped, games won, or a great E.R.A., it's all the same. We like being able to point to our stats.

Coming Up Short

Because I cannot keep a running tally of how well I'm doing as a dad, I tend to measure myself by how I fall short. Being a dad is probably the hardest thing I have ever done. I know it's important to have one-on-one time with each of my kids, to come home and forego turning on the "boob-tube" and vegging out. I need to get involved with them. I know that what I do at home is supposed to count for more than what I do at the office.

Why, then, does it seem so much easier to give of myself at work than it does at home?

I go into the office where I'm greeted by a stack of requests for me to call people suffering with cancer. I pick up the phone, make the calls, listen carefully, and try to respond with words of encouragement. Some time ago I came home after a day like that and Jonathan was complaining about not having any good friends in Colorado Springs as he had in Ohio. Did I listen carefully and respond with words of encouragement? Not really. I said, "Oh, stop your whining. You have plenty of friends."

Now remember, this is coming from the lips of a man who does a lot of public speaking. I go out in front of thousands of people (it feels good to be able to count something) and say, "My family is more important than my work. What I give to my kids and my wife is the most important thing in my life." Sometimes I feel like a hypocrite because while I'm out there saying one thing, I immediately go home and do another. People look at me and say, "Oh man! You're such a wonderful guy." And inside I'm thinking, *If you only knew.*

Another confession: Whenever I get in a plane to travel to some speaking engagement, I wonder if I'm going to die in a crash. Only then do I take a mental tally of all the things I should have done with my kids that I haven't done. In my head, I know my kids don't judge me by comparing what I've done with all the great things I've thought of doing (but never actually did) with them. But in my heart, that's what haunts me every time I fly.

The point is, if I tried to measure my worth as a dad based on my "performance," I don't think I'd like what I came up with. My numbers would be down, along with my spirits. I'd focus on my deficits rather than my assets and wind up believing my worth hovered somewhere between zero and negative three—not exactly All-Star numbers.

That's a problem, because I want to be in the Dad's Hall of Fame. I have shelves full of books telling me what to do to be a great dad, a real superstar. Yeah! That's what I want to be. I wrack my brains, thinking about the grand things I could do. Yet I have found that such things only distract me from the every-day things my kids appreciate most. It may feed my ego by try-ing to be a superstar, but my kids are not impressed.

Great, But Nothing Special

The other day, Tiffany was at the kitchen table working on her homework. I could have flipped on the TV and told her to go up to her room to work, but instead I looked over her shoulder and said, "Hey, can I help you do your homework?"

"Dad," she said with a touch of exasperation in her voice, "this is *math*. You know Mom's the only one who can help."

"Yeah, but I'm here. If you want me to try, I'll give it a shot," I said.

She kind of laughed and shook her head, but I could tell she appreciated my offer even as she replied, "Thanks anyway, Dad."

Now, there's no way I can measure her appreciation for my concern, but it counts for a lot. My "worth" to my daughter isn't measured by my ability to divide, subtract, or find the square root of some evil number. When she knows her dad is interested in her and her success, his "worth" in her eyes goes off the chart.

Jonathan's favorite thing in the world is going to the bat-ting cages with me. Last week I came home from work feeling good, but I discovered after walking in the door that Jonathan hadn't finished his chores. I could have blown up about it, but instead I said, "Let's get everything taken care of here and then we'll go down to the batting cages."

He got in gear and finished his chores in no time. Then we went to the batting cages, where I gave him some honest praise and coached him a bit. On the way home, we swung through Dairy Queen. With a big grin on his face and ice cream dripping from his mouth, he said, "Thanks, Dad." That was a great time, even though it was nothing special.

Incidents like these show me that while there are a lot of great ideas out there about what we might do with our kids, the bottom line is that they just want *us*. They don't care much what kind of package it comes in, as long as it comes with love. That's all that really matters . . . even if it can't be measured statistically.

"What My Dad Meant to Me"

In two earlier chapters I told part of the story of Jim Andrews, the man who died of melanoma in the summer of 1994. Jim meant a great deal to me in the six weeks I was privileged to know him. He was a great husband and a wonderful father.

Jim left behind three sons: Daniel (age 13), Taylor (age 12), and Kevin (age 8). While Jim was heartbroken at the thought that he would have to leave his wife and boys, he treasured the last moments he had with them. Jim used his final days to write a letter to his boys in which he talked about his faith and his hopes for their futures. He gave them advice and tried to sum up his life and his love in a matter of pages. Jim died a few weeks after he completed his letter. His boys are grateful for that precious manuscript, to which Jim committed his last thoughts and feelings for them. That gave them something tangible to hold on to after their dad passed away. More than just Jim's last letter, they will also carry with them the memories of what their dad gave them.

As I was thinking about this book, I thought I might be able to learn something about the worth of a dad by asking Jim's boys to describe what their dad meant to them. Sometimes I think we have to ask someone other than the man himself about what he's "worth." The following reflections were written almost a year after Jim died. Here's what Daniel, Taylor, and Kevin had to say (without any guidance from me or their mom):

My Memories of Dad (by Daniel, now 14)

- Racquetball at the Sheraton.
- When he was sick, he was available to talk.
- I want to be like him.
- He was respected by almost everybody.
- He was a good husband and a good dad.
- He cared about us more than he cared about himself.
- My dad was a Promise Keeper.
- He loved my mom with all his heart.
- Dad was never bitter about being sick.
- He wrote the letter to me and my brothers.

Written by Taylor (now age 13)

My dad was very special to me. He loved me, my mom, and my brothers more than anything in the world. I loved him the same way. He showed me he loved me by every night putting me to bed and praying with me.

When he was dying, he wrote the most incredible letter to me and my brothers. In it he repeatedly said he loved me.

Almost any man can be a father, but it takes a true man to be a dad. My dad was even better.

Written by Kevin (now age 9)

My dad ment love. Some of the things I loved most were that he cared enuf of us that he would come home from work. Then he would spend as much Time as he could. Almost every night he would take me to bed and he would prey and tuck us in bed. I also liked when he would wresel with us. Those things meant alot to me. that's some of the reasons I like my Dad!*

—Kevin

---

*I made no corrections to spelling or grammar. I think you will understand what the boy is trying to say.

Such simple words to sum up what a dad means to his kids. Nothing spectacular, nothing out of reach—just a man taking time to love his family. These letters convince me not only that Jim understood his true worth as a man, but that he did his level best to show his kids and his wife how much *they* were worth as well. It is worth noting that none of Jim's boys talked about the extraordinary, superhuman things Jim might have done for them—they simply and sweetly remembered the man. Not his performance, but the man himself.

Maybe it's not as complicated as we think?

Charlotte's Web and Shared Tears

Remember the two guys from chapter 1 whom I met on the plane going to Sacramento? Eventually we got around to talking about our kids, and "Tom" told a touching story about himself and his nine-year-old daughter.

He and his little girl were sitting together one night as he read her *Charlotte's Web*. At the end of the story, Charlotte (the spider who saves the life of Wilbur, the pig) dies. Tom said that when he read the ending, he and his daughter both started crying and sniffling. He stepped back to wipe his tears away, then apologized to his daughter. "Honey," he said, "I am so sorry for crying in front of you."

She looked into his eyes and replied, "Daddy, that's okay. When you cry with me, at least I know you are here."

That's perfect! Tom's tears proved to his daughter that he was right there with her in the middle of the story. His mind wasn't wandering off somewhere or drifting back to work. He wasn't thinking about finding a cure for cancer, which is what he does for a living. His tears were a sign to his little girl that he had shared the story and the moment with her.

Fleeting, precious moments like that can teach us far more about our "worth" than can thousands of hours spent in trying to "perform." Our kids don't want us to be strong as much as they want us to be there, with them, in heart and soul and mind and spirit—and sometimes with tears.

Just Sittin' Around the Barbecue Pit With You

The fellow on the aisle, "Fred," was going through a messy divorce. He said he would love to get back together with his wife, but he knew that was not going to happen unless they both got some serious help. In the meanwhile, he's been trying to "be there" for his kids. He's in the business of putting on seminars, but he canceled everything on his schedule so he could spend more time with his kids.

"I'm tired of this," he confessed. "I've been so focused on my work that I lost sight of my family. You know what really blew my mind? Whenever I go to spend time with my kids, I tell them we can do whatever they want to do. I guess I was willing to compensate for the pain they were going through because of the divorce. My time with them is limited, so I wanted our time to be special. You know what they say? They say, 'Dad, we just want to go back into the backyard and sit down around the barbecue pit and cook hot dogs with you.'"

Fred was willing to do anything . . . and his kids thought the most important thing he had ever done for them was to build a backyard fire pit, surrounded by a simple bench. When their family was intact, they would all sit back there on that little bench and cook hot dogs or roast marshmallows over the fire in the pit. That meant more to them than anything else their dad could do. Why? Because the activity itself was so amazing? No. It's because their dad was with them, having fun. That's it!

"I've been looking at my life and realizing that all the 'important' stuff I've been doing doesn't amount to a hill of beans," Fred continued. "What really matters in life is going into the backyard and cooking hot dogs with my children."

Fred's story backs up what we have just been talking about. We don't have to drum up super-spectacular ideas of fabulous things to do with our kids. That's not what gives us worth. We don't have to perform in order to earn our worth (or even to get our kids to recognize it). I have found that it doesn't matter too much what we do with our kids, as long as we are *with* them fully when we are with them in body. That is what is most important.

What Will They Remember?

People talk about building memories. What father doesn't want to build lasting, positive memories with his children? Eventually our kids are going to leave home, and the memories they carry with them will take on great importance. What will our kids say about us after they leave the nest and after we're gone? We don't have to do something spectacular to make a special memory for our kids. What we must do is to love them and be there 100 percent with them when we are present.

That's what it means to live out your worth as a man. That's how your kids will see the unbelievable worth that God has already built into you. Of course, should you mess up in this area of your life and lose your kids somewhere along the way, you won't lose your worth as a man—but believe me, you will make it a lot harder for your kids to believe in their own worth. And you will have an even harder time convincing yourself that you are worth half a confederate dollar.

A man who understands his God-given worth and who lives it out is giving his kids the richest treasure imaginable. And it's a lot easier than most of us think. We don't have to be supermen. We don't have to plan expensive, exotic vacations. We don't have to perform up to some excessive and exhaustive level. We just have to let our kids know that we love them. We have to be with them, really be with them. That's it. Shucks, even Dave Dravecky can do that.

Dad, I'm Glad Your Arm Is Gone

Not too long ago our family got together with some friends. We all put on our jeans, cowboy boots, and hats, and then we went horseback riding through the high country near Boulder, Colorado. After the ride, we spent a few hours eating good food and talking and laughing with our friends. As we prepared to leave, we meandered toward the front yard, talking all the way. Meanwhile, the kids restlessly waited for us to get in the car.

While I was trying to talk, Tiffany started hugging me. She is thirteen and not quite sure if she's Daddy's little girl or an independent young woman, but I still love those moments when she's my little girl (even if she is almost as tall as her mother). Tiffany stood on my left side, wrapped her arms around my neck, and snuggled her face next to mine.

"You know, Dad," she said softly, "I'm kinda glad your arm is gone. That way I can get closer to you." Then she smiled her big, beautiful smile and planted a kiss on my cheek.

Wow! Tiffany doesn't care how much money I used to make with that left arm or how hard I could throw a baseball. All she cares about is getting close to me. That blows me away. What she values most is whatever allows her to snuggle up to me.

You know, that's what your kids want, too. You may be working your tail off, trying to give them what you think they want, when all they really want is you—and your love.

Dads, we don't have to perform to gain our worth. Not in our jobs, not with our wives, and certainly not with our kids. I could spend several more pages trying to prove that to you from the Bible, but I don't have to.

I have a thirteen-year-old's kiss on my cheek that gives me all the proof I need.

Chapter Twelve

Man to Man

Eric Show and I were teammates on the San Diego Padres back in 1984. He was a Christian who pulled me toward a more committed relationship with God. Eric was the one who instilled within me the desire to be bolder with my faith. He encouraged me to talk about the living Jesus to whom I had given my life. Eric was a good friend to me, and he had a strong, positive impact on my life.

Yet on March 16, 1994, Eric Show was found dead in his bed at a drug rehab center, his life snuffed out by an overdose of heroine and cocaine. What went wrong? How could it have happened? It was such a sad, pointless waste. Eric had so much going for him—how could he have met his end at the point of a needle?

I think a lot about my old friend, and I believe one reason for Eric's collapse was that he never allowed himself to show his weakness. He never once talked to me about his struggles with sin or let on that he needed help. When he spoke to me, he was strong in his faith, almost to the point of being dogmatic. I now realize that Eric lived in hiding, trying to keep up an image that matched what he knew to be right. Maybe he didn't want to disillusion me, since he led me to a deeper faith in God; or maybe he thought I would reject him if I knew about his struggles. Whatever his reasons, Eric lived and died in hiding.

Lost Opportunities

After I left the Padres, I lost touch with Eric. Over the years I heard that he had a drug problem and that he had been in and out of several treatment programs, but we never mentioned it when we crossed paths. We kept things on a surface level.

Early in 1994, when I was speaking in Kentucky, Eric showed up in the crowd after I spoke. It was so good to see his face again. We talked a little, though not about anything of substance. He didn't mention that he was staying in a drug treatment facility in the area and I didn't pry. It was the last time I would see my friend this side of heaven.

Eric never knew how much he meant to me; that is a real tragedy. I wish I would have told him. Eric Show had great worth as a man and tremendous value in my life, but he never knew how much the real man—even with all his faults—meant to me. I think that kind of affirmation could have helped him, but I never told him. I deeply regret that now.

When Eric died of a drug overdose, the papers made a big deal out of it, and I can see why. The guy was a professional baseball player who made a public profession of faith in Jesus Christ. Pointing out how far he fell short of being a role model as a ballplayer or as a Christian made great copy. His character was always being blasted. In the eyes of the world, this guy was a radical, a controversial person, the guy who sat sullenly on the mound when Pete Rose got the record hit off of him to break Ty Cobb's record.

But you know what I saw when I was with Eric? I saw a man who would take the shirt off his back to give to a bum on the streets, then take him to a restaurant and buy him dinner. I saw Eric do a lot of things like that.

Eric's death was a personal loss to me because he was my friend. I knew he was troubled, and I certainly do not condone drug use. But Eric was a friend to me when I needed one most.

What I gained from our friendship still impacts my life today. Eric challenged me to be more than what I was. The Christian ideals he held up are still a standard for me, even though Eric didn't always live up to them himself.

Eric's value to me had nothing to do with a good slider or a good sinker. It had everything to do with what he gave me off the field as a friend: He gave me himself. He invested time in my life when he didn't have to. That mattered to me. Believe me, I didn't offer this guy intellectual stimulation. Eric was widely recognized as a multitalented near-genius who read and discussed the likes of Kant, Hegel, Marx, Freud, and Kierkegaard. Our friendship seemed one-sided because he was always giving to me when I felt like I had little to give back. At that time I needed a friend, and Eric Show was there for me.

There are so many things I wish I would have said to Eric but never did: that he was precious to me, that his failures didn't wipe out his worth as a man, that he didn't have to hide from me what was going on in his life.

It's too late now to change anything with Eric, but I can put into practice what I've learned from his life. I can tell others how precious they are to me. I can offer acceptance instead of criticism. I can be honest about my struggles with sin and affirm the worth of others, despite their struggles. Whenever another man dares to open up his struggles and failures with me, I won't criticize. I will encourage him that he has great worth, regardless of what he has done or what kind of shameful behavior has him trapped.

But perhaps most of all, I am determined to develop friendships with a few other men with whom I can openly share my heart. Eric didn't have that, and it cost him his life.

The Gift of a Burden Shared

Men today seem to be giving a lot of lip service to the idea of sharing their burdens with each other, but more often than not they are willing to listen to the burdens of others but not share their own. My friend Bob Knepper was always telling other men, including me, how important it was to be open and transparent. He was always the one who encouraged others to talk while he listened. That was his role. We all knew we could go to Bob anytime we had a burden. Bob believed in burden *bearing*, but he had a harder time with burden *sharing*.

Recently I noticed that Bob was obviously going through something difficult. His demeanor changed, and he was clearly struggling with some major issue in his life. Quite frankly, I wanted to know what was going on, but he was silent.

Eventually he did spill his guts. When I asked him why he never opened up with me before, he said, "I never felt a need to open up. Superficially, I never sensed the need for a close friend. With the exception of a few guys, I didn't have a friend I could lean on; so I convinced myself that I didn't need that kind of friendship. That was probably a self-defense mechanism. Throughout my baseball career, I tried to remain self-sufficient. Intellectually, I knew I needed a friend, but I convinced myself I had that with my buddies, although I never got to the point of opening myself up to them. The other night when I opened up with you was a first for me. Before that I never let my friends see what was going on inside of me."

Bob later told me that he had long sensed I wanted him to share his burdens with me, but he had a list of good reasons for not doing so. His reasons are probably the same ones lots of men cite for not opening up to their friends. Do any of them sound familiar?

- *I don't feel a need to open up.* Bob knew I wanted him to open up to me, but he never sensed the need. It felt good for him to be the one listening, so he kept going back to what felt good.
- *My background has taught me to get by without burdening anyone else with my problems.* Bob acknowledged that he had hurts and frustrations, but he had learned that it wasn't right to sit there and whine to somebody about them. He just accepted that he was "the kind of guy" who did the listening instead of the talking about personal problems.

- *I admit there may be an element of pride involved.* Bob knew I was willing to help bear his burdens and that I would have accepted him, but telling himself that he didn't need that kind of support put him a step above the rest of us. He didn't consciously think such a thing, but it felt good to believe he was the helper rather than the one who needed support.
- *I have always tried to be strong because I don't want to burden anyone with my weaknesses, struggles, or hurts.* Bob didn't want to weigh me down. He thought that sharing his burdens would only make problems for me. But sharing a burden doesn't make it twice as heavy; it makes it twice as light.

When Bob finally opened up, it had the opposite effect of what he feared. It was awesome! I hadn't sat and listened for so long and kept my mouth shut that much since we began meeting regularly over a year before. Instead of weighing me down with his burdens, he built me up by sharing them. His open heart wasn't a burden; it was an incredible gift! Our relationship took a major step forward in that instant. I thought, *FINALLY! Thank you! Thank you that you have said something about your struggles in your life, instead of me always being a burden to you!*

I finally realized that maybe, just maybe, this guy really did need me—which gave me a greater sense of my worth as a man. When he came to me and willingly shared his deepest thoughts and poured his heart out to me, it told me that he valued me enough to entrust me with something of great value: the whole person, not just the cover of strength.

One important way we affirm the value of our friends is to admit our need for them. We need to take turns affirming each other by bearing each other's burdens. Bob never understood that until he opened up, and neither will you. If you are merely giving lip service to the idea of sharing your burdens with another man, it's time to put the idea into practice. They will probably even thank you for it!

Being Part of the Team

One of the things I miss most about baseball is not being part of the team. There's a feeling of acceptance and confidence that comes from belonging to a team, especially a winning team. After I broke my arm while pitching in Montreal, I still suited up for every game and sat in the dugout with the Giants. Even though I hated not being able to play, it meant a lot to me just being part of the team.

What's so great about being part of a team? You are chosen. You are important because other guys depend on you to play your position; they need you. Something powerful happens to your sense of worth when you look at a group of men you respect and honestly think, *I'm one of them*. You are an accepted part of something bigger than yourself.

After I could no longer be a useful part of a baseball team, I began thinking more seriously about the value of belonging to a team. Not being part of a team has a powerful impact on the way a man sees himself. I'm not just talking about sports; I'm talking about feeling as if you are not a useful and accepted part of any group. Whether it's the scrawny kid at school who nobody picks during P.E. or the man rejected by his peers at work, not being part of a team undermines a guy's sense of his worth as a man. Can a man who suffers rejection like this from other men feel confident in his own worth? That's got to be tough.

Now that I'm not as active as I was when I was playing baseball, I've put on a few extra pounds (okay, maybe more than a few). Today I can imagine the damage that would be done if a group of guys, whose acceptance I valued, decided that physical fitness was going to be the criteria for whether I was "in."

I am firmly convinced that a little acceptance from other men goes a long way toward helping a man sense the tremendous worth built into him by God. I know how much it meant to me to have my teammates and other men affirm me when I could no longer cut it in baseball. I want to extend that same kind of acceptance to everyone I meet, regardless of his race, financial status, political persuasion, religious affiliation, appearance, or any other criterion. The worth of a man is found in the man, not in his externals or whether he can qualify for a particular team. I want to affirm that with every man I meet.

Pitchers and Their Catchers

I am convinced that many men have never grasped their true worth because they have never been accepted by and been in real sync with another man whom they considered an intimate friend. It's amazing how much a friendship like this can teach a guy.

I have pitched to some good catchers, but there was always something special about my relationship with Terry Kennedy when we played together with the San Diego Padres. Something magical happened when I was on the mound and TK was behind the plate. It's one thing to pitch to a player who is a good catcher; but you go to another level when you pitch to a catcher you click with. TK and I clicked.

The winter before I made my comeback, Terry was a member of the Baltimore Orioles. I didn't know for sure whether I would be able to make a comeback or, if I did make it back, when it would happen. One thing I did know for sure: If I made a comeback, there was only one guy I wanted behind the plate on that day. While I was going through therapy to get back in shape, I was seriously praying that TK would get traded to the Giants. The winter of 1988–1989, TK *was* traded to the Giants and became the back-up catcher in time for my comeback game, August 10, 1989.

The day before I was scheduled to pitch, I went into the office to talk to Roger Craig, my manager. I said, "Look, I don't care what you say, Roger—TK is my catcher!"

"Don't worry, Dave," Roger replied. "He's already penciled in."

It amazed me to see how things came about so that TK was there for me when I needed him most. I took that as a definite answer to prayer.

It's a big deal to have the type of relationship with a catcher I had with Terry Kennedy. When I was on the mound and we got in sync, I would be thinking "fastball/slider" and he would put it down. Often it was almost as if I could turn my brain off because he was thinking with me. We got going in a groove together like a single unit.

Trust was essential in that relationship. I had to know that he knew me so well that he could pull the best out of me. We had faith in each other, confidence in each other's abilities, and unity. All of that is subconscious. I wasn't on the mound thinking, *I know TK has the same goals as I have.* When I was on the mound, I couldn't afford to stop and worry about the catcher's competence or wonder, *Is this guy really with me? Is his pitch selection right or wrong?* With TK, I never had to stop and think about anything other than the next pitch. I could have that singleness of focus because TK and I functioned as one unit.

Bob Knepper recalled watching me pitch to TK when we were all on the Giants together. He said, "Dave, I was envious because I never had that kind of relationship where I clicked with a catcher. I watched from the dugout and I could see it. I would have given my right arm to have that kind of a relationship with a catcher. You look at most great pitchers and somewhere early in their career, they had that kind of relationship with a catcher that really clicked.

"Throughout my career, I have had tons of catchers who were good, but I never really clicked with any one of them. I bet there were some games where I shook off fifty pitches. I'd want to throw a fastball; the catcher said no. I'd want to throw a slider; he'd shake me off. He'd put down a curveball; I'd shake him off. At that point I started wondering, *Maybe I'm throwing the wrong pitch.* Finally I'd get the change-up and by that time, there was no way to get a rhythm. We had been going back and forth so much it shook my confidence."

In life, if you are around people who are constantly shaking you off, disagreeing with you or challenging your judgment, there is no way to get in a rhythm and do your best. That's why every man needs to find at least one other man he clicks with, a friend who will get to know him well enough to pull the best out of him.

A rookie pitcher usually starts out wanting a catcher who will just catch. He doesn't want him to give input on what he's doing on the mound. The inexperienced pitcher thinks he can succeed on his own. He sees the catcher's input as interference. The seasoned pitcher not only allows the catcher to give him input, he appreciates it.

In every game there are times a pitcher is indecisive about what to throw. If he has to stop to think about a pitch, it interrupts his rhythm. He needs a catcher who knows him better than he knows himself, who knows what he can do in any given situation. The catcher has to size up the whole picture and then give his pitcher the benefit of his viewpoint.

At the times when we are indecisive in life, we need to have a guy on the field with us who has a broader perspective of our situation. We need him to know us, our tendencies, and our options, so he can help us make a good decision with the benefit of his objectivity.

Yet even when you click with your catcher, the two of you don't always agree on every pitch. There were times TK came out to the mound and said, "What's going on here, Dave? What are you thinking?" But because the relationship was built on trust and mutual respect, even confrontation didn't break my rhythm. We'd have that talk and come to some mutual understanding. Then I'd go to the pitch without losing my confidence. I knew I didn't have to go the way he called it, but because I had confidence in him, his call carried weight. It made me think, *Maybe I should go that way.*

In a solid friendship there's got to be confidence, acceptance, and mutual respect, not blind agreement on either side. When I know my friend believes the best about me, I can take whatever confrontation becomes necessary and it doesn't shake my confidence as a man. There is room for helpful negotiation without either man getting offended if the other doesn't do exactly what his friend thinks is best.

I have that kind of relationship with a few guys. When they offer advice, I'm neither pressured to follow it nor offended by it, and they know me well enough not to be offended if I don't choose their route. Often my friend's advice gets me to stop and contemplate my decision, then go to God and ask him what he thinks I should do. I make better decisions when I have a trusted friend who feels free to give me his viewpoint; sometimes it causes me to change my mind, other times I become more convinced that the choice I have made is the right one. And sometimes I learn later that I should have listened to my friend's advice in the first place!

Every man can benefit from finding a friend with whom he clicks. Lots of guys go through life without that kind of friendship; I think of Eric Show again. What a shame. It's important to find somebody with whom you can develop a long-term relationship. We ought to pray that God will bring us together with the right men and help us develop relationships where we click.

I guess if God cared enough to get a particular catcher traded to a particular ball club for a particular game (which turned out to be the most important game of my life), he cares enough to help us find a few men with whom we can click, whose friendship can help us in all of life.

What I Learned From Mickey Mantle

What can a friend mean in your life? The example of Mickey Mantle suggests an answer.

Without a doubt, Mickey Mantle was one of the all-time great baseball players. As a kid who dreamed of being a ballplayer, one of my heroes was Mickey Mantle. He was living out the dream I hoped to accomplish one day. I am sure that by watching him as a kid, I was inspired in ways that helped my game. Yet without a doubt, I learned more about the worth of a man from Mickey's final days on this earth than I ever learned from him about baseball.

An article by Bob Briner—a friend, the president of Pro-Serv Television, and author of several books—describes how Mickey spent his last days.[1] How you spend your final hours says volumes about what you consider worthwhile in this life and what is of utmost importance. When the end approached, Mickey didn't call all his old teammates. He didn't call his old drinking buddies. He didn't call anybody to come over and rehash his career as a baseball player. Instead, he called together his family and one other man, Bobby Richardson. When Mickey looked back over his life and all the people he had ever known, Bobby Richardson was the one man he wanted by his side as he lay dying.

Bobby Richardson was his teammate on the New York Yankees during the 1950s. Bobby played second base and professed faith in Jesus Christ. When the other guys were hanging out together, drinking and carousing, Bobby didn't join them. Mantle had labeled him "the milk drinker." Bobby didn't brag about being a Christian. He simply played the game, loved God, tried to walk with integrity, offered the hope of heaven to his friends, and was always available to his friend Mickey throughout the years.

Over the long haul, Bobby Richardson's life backed up his profession of faith and proved his love for his friend. That's why he was the one called to be with Mickey at the end. *The New York Times* reported that Bobby led his friend to saving faith in Jesus Christ. A few weeks before he died, Mickey told the world's press corps that he wanted to be remembered as a model of what *not* to do in life. Regret and remorse were etched all over his sunken features. Yet at the end, Bobby Richardson was able to show Mickey that, in Christ, he had unbelievable worth as a man. Mickey died with a ravaged body, but with a redeemed and priceless soul.

No one can deny the value Mickey Mantle had as a baseball player, but that value would have meant nothing if he had perished eternally. The eternal worth of Mickey's soul was established on his deathbed when he recognized Jesus as his Savior and crossed safely over into eternal life. He never would have discovered that worth, however, had it not been for a faithful friend, Bobby Richardson, "the milk drinker."

Faithful to the End

I am so glad that God doesn't measure the worth of a man the same way the world does. The world tends to pile up all a man's faults and failures on one side of the scale and all his good deeds on the other. It weighs them out and says, "The bad outweighs the good, so this man wasn't worth anything." That's not how God does it. Sin is sin, no matter how socially unacceptable the sin may be. The blood of Jesus paid for it all and washes away every sin. For the man who accepts Jesus Christ as his Savior, all that remains on God's scales is the gold that is left after the sin disappears. God weighs only the gold.

Bobby Richardson didn't count his worth by how many speeches he gave as the president of Baseball Chapel. He didn't brag about how many players he led to the Lord. He didn't look for glory down here. He looked to be faithful, and his faithfulness paid off. He knows that he and his friend Mickey Mantle will see each other again.

I, too, want to be faithful over the long haul. I want my life to encourage my friends to turn to me when they need help. I want quietly to live out a life that exemplifies my values and makes me approachable to other men.

When I was a kid, I probably would have found it hard to believe that a milk-drinking second baseman who played in the shadow of a much more celebrated star would be the hero I wanted most to emulate. But that is exactly what has happened. Through hearing about what took place surrounding Mickey Mantle's death, Bobby Richardson has become my hero.

And now if you'll excuse me—I think I'll go get a glass of milk.

Notes

1. Bob Briner, *Contemporary Christian Music Magazine,* 18 (November 1995), p. 34. Bob is the author of *Roaring Lambs* and *Lambs Among Wolves.*

Part Three

Where I'm Headed

◆ ◆ ◆ ◆ ◆

Chapter Thirteen

Preparing for the Challenges Ahead

Life is filled with challenges. It was a challenge for me to become a professional baseball player. It was a challenge to try to make a comeback after cancer first attacked my arm. It was a greater challenge when I had to decide about what to do with my life after the amputation. And the challenges just keep on coming.

What is true for me is just as true for you—it's the same for all of us. The challenges vary from man to man, but we all face challenges of various kinds. They take on many forms and present unique problems for each of us, but one thing stays the same: They keep on coming day after day, month after month, year after year.

I think that's especially true for one of the greatest challenges that all men face. Each one of us, probably at several points throughout our lives, is going to face stiff challenges to our worth as men. Circumstances will occur and events will

155

unfold that will cause us to question the worth God has built into us. The question for us is, *How will we respond?*

In this chapter I want to look briefly at a few challenges that often cause us to question our worth. The following list is by no means exhaustive, but it does cover some of the most important challenges I have faced so far and most of us will face as the years roll on. In each case, the real challenge is to remember and to live out the incredible worth that God has built into each of us as men made in his image. If we can do that, I think we will be okay, regardless of the storms that might blow our way.

The Challenge of Starting Over

I am not the only guy on the block who has had to start over in life, but I certainly had a lot of it to do after playing professional baseball my entire adult life. Starting over for me involved launching out on a new career path, letting go of dependence on other people, and learning to stand on my own two feet. Challenges like that can cause a man to doubt his worth; at least, that's what happened with me.

When I was in baseball, I relied on other people for almost every aspect of my life. All I had to do was pitch. Beyond that, somebody else took care of every detail. They flew me where I was supposed to go, packed my bags, made arrangements for my room, and even gave me money for meals. I was making hundreds of thousands of dollars, and they were still giving me meal money! And when I came home, Jan took care of everything there. I was spoiled and didn't even know it.

When I got cancer and went through all of the medical problems, the staff at the hospital took care of me. We moved back to our hometown in Ohio to be near our families because I was sick and we needed help. There again, people who loved us willingly took care of me.

In my new writing and speaking career, I had a literary agent, a booking agent, and a publisher, all eager to help me and willing to make decisions for me. It was a different arena and a different phase of life, but it was the same story—allowing other people to direct my life. It felt safe that way because they all knew exactly what they were doing.

When Jan and I were in the midst of this major change in our lives, just before we found out I had to get my arm amputated, Dr. John Townsend referred us to a counselor. We didn't see John again until three months later. When we did meet at that time, he asked me, "Well, Dave, how does it feel to be three months old?"

That's when the truth struck me: I really was starting life over. I had a lot of growing up to do! And that realization did not do a lot for my sense of worth as a man.

When it came to taking full responsibility for my life and decisions, I was a baby. Like a little child learning to walk, I was trying to learn how to respond to a whole new set of experiences, the pain and suffering along with the joy and excitement of my new life. All kinds of wonderful things were happening along with all kinds of painful things, and I was trying my best to walk—but I felt as if I was stumbling and bouncing into walls each time I tried something new. My whole system had been turned upside down, and I felt very uncertain of myself. For Pete's sake, I was an adult. Why should a real man struggle with such life adjustments?

Taking responsibility for my life was one of the hardest things I have ever done. For us, starting over meant weaning ourselves from dependence on other people. We had been living in Ohio for five years. Jan and I both realized it was time to step out on our own to get a fresh start. It's not necessary to move to get a fresh start, but for us, moving to Colorado was an important part of beginning to make our own decisions. It was painful because we left friends and family whom we loved very much. Yet the move was in our best interest because we were too used to depending on others and it would have been easy to fall back into the old pattern. We had to take that step to mature and move forward.

In the realm of business, as the leader of our ministry, I still sometimes feel like a bumbling child. Sometimes I have to make decisions that my previous life didn't prepare me to make.

Whether my choices are right or wrong, I have to live with the consequences. I am trying to do my best, and that helps some. I am surrounded by a great support team, and that helps a lot. What helps most is knowing that God has allowed me this opportunity to start over and doesn't expect perfection. I believe he is using these challenges to mature me into the full stature of the man he knows I can become.

Sure, I could go back to letting other people take responsibility for my life. I know somebody else could probably do a better job of handling the things that are new for me. I make mistakes, and I hate feeling as if my mistakes might hurt other people. But whenever I feel that downward pull that tempts me to give up, I counter it with the realization that in some ways I'm just a baby. I'm learning and growing, and that's always a painful process. But as long as God has given me another chance at life, I figure I should do the best I can to grow into the opportunities he has given me.

I am still learning what this life is all about, but I know it's better to start over than to give up. There is great value in starting over, no matter how old you are, what you have lost, or how long you have been dependent on other people. The process of taking responsibility for my own life and decisions has presented a number of challenges to my worth as a man, but by working through those challenges, I have gained a greater sense of that worth than I ever enjoyed before.

The Challenge of the Missing Backup

Even though I just mentioned that Jan and I felt it was necessary to uproot ourselves from Ohio and move to Colorado if we were to stand on our own two feet, it's still true that everybody needs a friend to back them up should they get into trouble. Standing on your own two feet doesn't mean standing alone. No matter how big you are, there are times when you aren't big enough to handle alone what life throws at you. I know for a fact that Jan and I would not have made it through the past seven years if it were not for many people who backed us up in practical ways when we were in trouble.

Because that kind of backup is so important to us, one of the theme verses for our ministry says, "Let us not love with words or tongue but with actions and in truth" (1 John 3:18). That's why we don't simply talk to people who are hurting, we also send practical help—sometimes referrals to a support group, sometimes a basket of gifts that will help their particular situation. We might send the mother of a child suffering with cancer a gift basket of personal care items, because we have seen so many moms who stop taking care of themselves when their child is hospitalized. That's just a little thing, but a tangible form of help means more than mere words, any day of the week. And when you don't get it, you can start to feel worthless.

I remember a time when I was still in baseball that an argument broke out about having beer in the clubhouse. I thought I would speak up and voice my opinion. I felt confident doing so because I was surrounded by several Christian buddies who I knew shared my point of view. So I took a stand . . . and found myself all alone. Then one of my teammates who didn't appreciate my opinion challenged me to a fight. My Christian buddies just sat there like bumps on a log, looking at me with expressions that said, "Gosh, Dave, I can't believe you just said that!" I was thinking, *Thanks for all the support, boys!* I was up against a guy six feet, four inches, 240 pounds, who was about to kill me—and I had no backup! I got no support. I was all alone.

When you feel abandoned by a friend who says he cares but doesn't back you up, the bond between you and your friend is stripped away, tempting you to withdraw. Of course, when people fail to back us up, God will come through for us in some way; but that's not his ideal plan. God commands us to love each other. Those are not just sweet and sentimental words. True love is practical. A big part of loving each other is being there to back each other up when we are in trouble. We are not to withdraw from others just because no one was there to back *us* up when we needed *them*.

In baseball, if a hitter charges the mound after getting a brush-back pitch, it's the catcher's job to be on that hitter and stop him. The catcher is the first backup the pitcher has. Any catcher will back up his pitcher in that kind of situation because that's part of his job. But if somebody charged the mound when I was pitching and Terry Kennedy was behind the plate, TK would have been on that guy, not just because it was his job, but because it was me under attack. The two of us were a team. His actions came from both duty and relationship. That's a good picture of how we ought to back up those to whom we are committed, both family and friends.

You want a sure way to sense the worth God has already built into you? Then back up another man who is unjustly in trouble or under attack. Back up your kids when they are in trouble at school. Back up your pastor when he comes under criticism. Back up your neighbor when he needs some practical help. Back up your wife by helping around the house or doing something that helps her career.

That kind of practical support is the work of God in this world. It's part of the job description of a Christian, but it shouldn't be done out of mere duty. It should be done out of a heartfelt commitment to all those whom we say we love. In that way we turn a challenge to our sense of worth into an opportunity to sense that worth more deeply.

The Challenge of Man-to-Man Relationships

While there are great benefits in building solid friendships with other men, there are also risks. As in any venture in life, you only get the rewards if you take the risks. But you had better know what the risks are before you start out, or you may pay a higher price than is necessary.

In any relationship, there is always a risk of rejection. Suppose you dare to share something that comes from deep inside, only to be rejected because of what you said. How does that make you feel? Pretty awful. Sometimes the rejection is so painful that you begin to believe all sorts of negative things about who you are as a man. Rejection can greatly damage your sense of worth as a man.

So do you avoid relationships where you could be rejected? After all, as long as you keep them on a surface level, talking only about sports or work or the weather, you have nothing to lose. But if you should share your heart and then be rejected, *you* feel rejected. A book by John Powell titled *Why Am I Afraid to Tell You Who I Am?* answers the question posed in the book's title this way: "I am afraid to tell you who I am, because, if I tell you who I am, you may not like who I am, and it's all that I have."[1] That sums it up. There is real risk in entering into friendships that go beyond the surface level.

One man who had committed adultery turned to men in his church to help him put his life back together. These men knew and loved him and were supportive, kept his confidences, and affirmed his worth as a man while helping him work through some difficult areas of temptation. While most did not struggle with the same kinds of sexual temptation that he did, they treated his sin like their own, recognizing they were all prone to sin. This group built him up and helped him heal emotionally. They also encouraged him as he worked to rebuild the serious damage done to his family.

Then this man and his family moved to another part of the country. There they got involved in a church in which the leader of the men's group repeatedly invited the man to join. He took his time getting to know a few men, testing the waters to see if they seemed trustworthy. He finally decided to attend the men's group. He went a few times but didn't say much. The leader continued to be friendly, calling every week to invite him to attend the next. The man finally decided it was safe enough to venture out and confess what he had done, what he had been through, and how he had been working through the issues related to his fall. The men seemed cordial, but after that the men's ministry leader stopped calling. The man never asked whether this new coldness resulted from what he shared, but he decided not to risk further rejection by saying any more. He stopped going to the meetings, and to this day no one has called him back.

There are at least two lessons here. First, we must be ready for the possibility that the men with whom we discuss "difficult stuff" may not be prepared to handle it. If we are dealing with issues that are deeply disturbing, perhaps the best place to talk is with a professional counselor. Second, if a guy takes a major risk by sharing something potentially devastating, make sure you reassure him of your acceptance. The men's ministry leader who stopped calling may not have done so because of what the new man said; in fact, he may have been preoccupied with some entirely unrelated issue. But whenever a confession brings an obvious risk of rejection, you cannot go too far in reassuring the guy who opened his heart that he is still accepted.

Another risk is that the men to whom you reveal a confidence might later turn around and use your words against you. Greg, the pastor of a thriving church, gave me a good warning. "Be careful!" he said. "You can be too open. I have opened up, shared what was really going on inside me—and in doing so, I have given others the ammunition they needed to shoot me." Men can blow each other away, and they aren't just using air rifles or 30.06s; they're using cannons. That's why you have to consider whether the people you confide in might have some reason to use your words against you. Use discretion, and share deeply only with those who have proven their allegiance to you.

One last risk is that you may bare your soul, but if no one else opens up, you end up feeling foolish. That's how I was starting to feel in some of the groups I was part of. I got tired of always being the vulnerable one. You get to a point where you think, *I just don't know how much I want to let people in anymore.* And yet I know the value of letting people in.

Eventually I had to say how much I disliked always being the one who talked about what was going on inside. When we discussed how I felt about my openness not being reciprocated, I learned the others were letting me talk because that is what they thought I needed. Only when I spoke up did they realize I needed to be able to play a different role in the group.

That worked out well in my case, but it could have blown up in my face. I took a risk that the other guys might write me off. That's one of the risks, but that risk contains its own reward. When you are real and dare to share who you are with others, you may drive some men away—but the ones who stay are great prospects for deeper friendships.

The Challenge of Our Flesh

The story I'm about to tell is kind of crude, but there's a good lesson in it, so I want you to bear with me. It has to do with my phantom arm.

When part of your body is amputated, the receptors in the brain that once controlled that part still think there is a limb to command. You feel sensations where your missing limb used to be; you can feel an itch, but you can't scratch it. It's really weird. Shortly after my arm was amputated, I felt intense pain in my left arm and hand. It felt as if someone was holding a match at the end of my fingertips, but I couldn't put the fire out or draw my hand away from the flame. Other times it felt as if someone was trying to pry the nails off of my fingers. The phantom pain doesn't bother me as much as it once did, but I couldn't control it even if it did. This phantom part of me has a mind of its own.

I used to be able to move my phantom arm. If I concentrated hard, with no distractions, I could mentally straighten it out, raise it up, bring it down, and move it into a more comfortable position. During this time, Jan and I were at the mall, and she was getting all over my case about something. I was extremely angry with her, but I didn't want to say anything back to her in public. I just let her say her piece and then walked on ahead.

With her back turned, an urge came over me I found impossible to resist. I raised up my phantom arm and gave her one of those gestures that you might see when a driver cuts off another car in traffic. It's not the kind of gesture a Christian man should ever make toward his wife, but when you do it with a phantom arm and nobody can see you. . . .

Are you shocked that I would do such a thing? Well, I agree with you; it was shocking. It shocked me too (but not too much).

163

But it didn't reflect who Dave Dravecky really is in Christ. Every Christian has an ongoing wrestling match between the flesh and our true selves.

The funny part is that Jan turned around and caught me. With a look of disbelief on her face, she "saw" my invisible arm and finger . . . and just busted up laughing. "David!" she howled, "I know what you did! I know exactly what you did!" My face gave me away and I started busting up too.

While we stood there laughing, two sweet little ladies who had been walking just behind us came up and asked for my autograph. Jan could hardly contain herself—she caught the ironic difference between my public image and the actions of the old man of flesh. I wonder if those nice little ladies would have requested my autograph had they been able to see my phantom gesture? Probably not.

That taught me a good lesson, though. I would never flip my wife off, publicly or in private. Sure, I get mad at Jan and she gets mad at me. But I love Jan, and the real me would never treat her so crudely. There's a hidden part of me, however, that would. My unredeemed flesh has a mind of its own, and that mind is crude. If I let my flesh take control, it gets me into trouble by thinking and doing things the real Dave Dravecky hates.

I guess that's just part of being a member of the fallen human race. On this point I'm no different from the apostle Paul, who admitted that "nothing good dwells within me, that is, in my flesh" (Romans 7:18, RSV). Every guy on the planet has this same kind of struggle going on inside him. If he forgets who he truly is in Christ, he can quickly start believing all kinds of lies about himself and end up feeling worthless.

Paul himself admitted to the same kind of struggle, so I guess we're in good company. He said, "I do not understand what I do. For what I want to do I do not do, but what I hate I do" (Romans 7:15). He admitted his struggle and did not pretend to have it all together, yet he never doubted for a minute that God had truly changed him forever. Maybe we should follow his example.

Jesus said that we would know the truth and the truth would set us free. If we men became more honest about the depth of the evil that dwells in our flesh, I think we would have more freedom from bondage to things we think and do that offend the new men we have become in Christ.

The Challenge of Receiving

Men don't like to receive; they like to earn. Yet as long as we refuse to receive, we won't grow. God is not interested in hiring us as his servants. He'd rather adopt us as his children. There's a big difference between those two.

My friend Chris Bingaman said he learned a valuable lesson about the necessity of receiving when he was battling cancer. He described it this way:

> Immediately after my diagnosis with cancer I was covered with people's expressions of kindness. I received everything from cards, flowers, meals, babysitting help, and money. I was placed on every local prayer chain and received a lot of calls to let me know people were praying for me daily.
>
> As my battle with cancer became more evidently long term and people became aware that I was going to need a bone marrow transplant, the gifts from people's hearts only became more generous. I saw people in our community who didn't make half as much per year as I did bring me food and money.
>
> This was one of the most difficult things I ever experienced as a man. Being in a successful family business, I was used to giving to others. I was familiar with people coming to me for help. Never in my wildest dreams did I imagine I would need help from others. The more I experienced this generous outpouring of help, the more and more uncomfortable I became being on the receiving end. I truly believe that for most men it is easier to be in a position to give rather than to have to receive.
>
> At first, I didn't know how to say thanks. Every time someone did something to show their concern, I didn't know how to adequately express my heartfelt appreciation.

THE WORTH OF A MAN

Also, I didn't like the feeling of receiving a free gift. As people did things for me, I wrote it down with the intention that someday I would pay them back. However, as my battle with cancer stretched from months to years, I gave up trying to keep an account of everything I thought I owed everyone.

Finally, the Lord spoke to my heart about this issue of receiving. I think as a man you subconsciously want to feel that you have earned everything you have. I took pride in being financially self-sufficient. Being on the receiving end made me realize that even the things I previously earned came through the generous gifts of God—gifts of opportunity and ability. As I reflected on this humbling experience, another thought became clear to me. The greatest gift I ever received is salvation. And there isn't one thing I have ever done or ever could do to help earn or pay back what our Savior has given me.

I knew that the Bible said we are saved by grace through faith and not by our works. But somehow, I subconsciously felt that all I was doing was helping make me a worthy recipient of God's grace. What a misconception that was! But as a man, receiving something I have not earned is hard.

Chris is right. It is difficult for men simply to receive a gift, especially if that gift is more expensive than they can afford. But receiving is the only way we can discover and experience our full worth as men. The only way a man can be saved is by receiving the love of the Father as a gift. The Bible says the only thing we can earn from God through our own efforts is condemnation and death (Romans 6:23). But it also says, "For it is by grace you have been saved, through faith—and this not from yourselves, it is the gift of God—not by works, so that no one can boast" (Ephesians 2:8–9).

I have had to learn to receive, and it hasn't been easy. But it sure has been worth it.

They Just Keep Coming

Count on it: For the rest of your life, you will face challenges to your worth as a man. You will, and so will I. But we can also rest in the knowledge that for every challenge there is both an answer and the opportunity to live out more fully the great worth God has placed in each of us.

One bit of wisdom that has helped me do this is contained in the following quote by Chuck Swindoll. When I speak, I often use it. I believe every word he says here. I remind myself of these truths whenever I am tempted to get discouraged by the big challenges I face, and I am hoping it will help you as much as it helps me.

Attitude

The more I live, the more I realize the impact of attitude on life. Attitude, to me, is more important than facts. It is more important than education, than money, than circumstances, than failures, than successes, than what other people think or say or do. It is more important than appearance, giftedness or skill. It will make or break a company . . . a church . . . a home. The remarkable thing is we have a choice every day regarding the attitude we will embrace for that day. We cannot change our past. We cannot change the fact that people will react in a certain way. We cannot change the inevitable. The only thing we can change is our attitude . . . I am convinced that life is 10% what happens and 90% how I react to it.[2]

Will facing these challenges be easy? Hardly. Sometimes it will be a real struggle. But the nice thing about a struggle is, we can win. And with Christ living inside us, how could we wind up as anything but champions?

Notes

1. Powell, John, *Why Am I Afraid to Tell You Who I Am?* (Chicago: Argus Communications, 1969).

2. Cf. Charles Swindoll, *Strengthening Your Grip: Essentials in an Aimless World* (Waco, Tex.: Word, 1982), p. 206.

Chapter Fourteen

One Comeback After Another

Do you remember the story of Scott O'Grady, the United States Air Force pilot shot down over Bosnia in June 1995? Because his mission was dangerous, O'Grady had been required to prepare for the possibility that he might go down in enemy territory. As a part of his training, he spent six days alone in the rugged terrain of Washington State, learning survival tactics. He learned to find water and food and to identify edible plants and even bugs in order to stay alive.

When O'Grady flew his sorties over Serb-held territories, his standard issue included a survival kit. Inside was water, a first-aid kit, a compass, flares, a pistol, survival guidelines, an evasion map, a radio, batteries, and a few other essentials. His superiors wanted him and all his fellow pilots to be prepared for an emergency.

When O'Grady's F–16 fighter jet was torn in two by a surface-to-air missile, the Bosnian Serbs watched him eject and tracked his open parachute as it drifted down. He had only four minutes to dispose of his parachute and burrow his body into the ground with only his camouflage gear showing before the Serbs were beating the bushes looking for him. Had he not learned survival principles before he was shot down, he could not have evaded capture. The principles he learned in advance kept him alive until he could be rescued.

O'Grady knew that although he was on the ground by himself, he was not alone. He was part of the NATO armed forces and a member of the United States Air Force. He also trusted that God was with him. With his radio he communicated with his friends, out there somewhere, who were prepared to come to his rescue. With prayer he sent out a signal to God, asking for help. Both connections were vital to his survival.

For six days O'Grady survived in enemy territory, evaded capture, and finally sent out a signal that told his buddies, "I'm alive. Help!" Immediately the Air Force called out the Marines and within hours, forty aircraft, under cover of a NATO AWACS radar plane, came to his rescue. They pulled him onto a helicopter and sped him back to safety, through enemy fire. He was shivering, dehydrated, and suffering from exposure. He was given a canteen of water and an MRE (meal, ready-to-eat), and the commander ordered two young Marines to flank him, sharing their warmth to restore his body heat. It was a remarkable rescue and an amazing story.

The Worth of a Man has something in common with O'Grady's story. Just as the Air Force's survival principles helped keep O'Grady physically alive, so this book has tried to be a kind of survival manual to help men overcome the struggles of discovering and living out their worth as men.

How do we survive with a sense of our worth intact when we get shot down in life? We have looked at a few specific challenges in the last chapter, but in this one I want to say basically just one thing: Hang in there. It can be a struggle, but don't give up. There will be times when things will look bad, but if you have learned some survival principles and are sending out messages for help, you can make it out alive. Just keep going.

You might even say life is just one comeback after another.

A Jock, a Hero, a Guy Who Needs the Grace of God

Who am I? That's a tough question. Who are you? If you are anything like me, the list of words that one group of people would use to describe who you are probably contradicts the list another group might develop. I think that's part of being human.

Most people think of me as a jock, a professional athlete. It is hard for people to relate to a jock unless they are one too. Being a professional athlete has great rewards, but it can be tough in some ways. You are put out there in the limelight, and there is a ton of pressure on you to perform on the field. You are expected to be a role model for kids—and you want to be—so you try to live up to that image off the field as well. You are supposed to live up to expectations that are more demanding than most people will ever know. Such expectations are even tougher to live up to when you face struggles that people don't want to believe you have.

I walked into a Christian bookstore the other day and saw a rack of books called "Today's Heroes." One of those books had my name and face on the cover. Is that who I am? One of today's heroes? That's okay, I guess. We need people to look up to in life, and if I can encourage others through being a hero of sorts, that's great.

But there's more to me than just the jock or today's hero. I have problems like everyone else, and I don't always deal with them well. I am a guy who struggles every day. I struggle with being down, with being a husband, with communicating, and with how to lead a ministry. Every time I turn the corner, I find another problem in front of me that I don't know how to deal with. I look at my life and I say to myself, "Is this the way it's going to be, day after day after day?" And the answer is, probably.

I believe in being the best I can be at whatever I do. I continually evaluate who I am and what my life is about to make sure I am being the best I can be. Yet I have come to realize that it takes time to grow up, no matter how old you are—and I'm still growing up. I'm learning that I can endure this journey and the ongoing struggles best when I accept that I am a man who has faults and a man who is still in the process of learning and growing toward maturity. Life is more manageable when I realize it calls for one comeback after another.

Lions and Giants and Bears, Oh My!

The Bible tells a story about a guy who was a jock, a national hero, and also a sinner. In a strange sort of way, that comforts me. He was a guy who had to depend on the grace of God, just like me. This man, David, fought bears and lions—and won. He won the greatest slingshot competition of all time, where the prize was more than just the pennant. The fate of his entire country depended on how well he could pitch a little stone toward the massive forehead of a giant named Goliath. When he beaned that Giant (who was fortunately from Philistia, not San Francisco), he became an instant hero. The whole country was cheering him, honoring him, loving him. I know how heady it can be to receive that kind of applause and the love of an entire nation. It's overwhelming—so overwhelming that it can go to your head.

David was far from a perfect guy. I am so relieved that the Bible doesn't hide how much of a sinner David could be. It comforts me to see how much this guy messed up. He had it all: He became king; he was famous; he had tons of money; he was a skilled and successful warrior. He even had a great relationship with God, leading the entire nation in worship through his songs. But one day he caught a glimpse of his neighbor's wife as she was stepping in and out of the tub. He liked what he saw and had an affair with her. When he found out she was pregnant, he had her husband killed to try to keep his image intact. David kept up the pretense until he was confronted with what he had done.

When he finally realized his sin wasn't quite as secret as he thought it was, he admitted his failures and came clean. He wrote a couple of songs about what happened inside him while he was trying to keep up the image. One of them is found in

Psalm 51, in which he says, "Create in me a pure heart, O God, and renew a steadfast spirit within me. . . . Restore to me the joy of your salvation and grant me a willing spirit, to sustain me" (verses 10, 12).

You know, whoever I am and whatever labels I use to describe myself, I don't want to live in deceit. I would rather be real, even if it tarnishes the image. I want to be real, even though it means I have to admit some ugly things about myself. Whoever I am, I will always be a guy who needs the grace of God. When I realize God's grace in my life and who I am in relationship to him, that gives me the will to live for him every day, trying to be my personal best, but also honest about my faults and failures.

I have told you some things in this book that may have surprised you—they don't match my public image. I hope you didn't mind or hold it against me. I did not do it for shock value, but in hopes that you will be encouraged to see the grace of God at work in the life of a man just like you. I hope it encourages you to come clean with God and receive his grace that erases all our faults and failures. And most of all, I hope it motivates you to keep on plugging, because life really is just one comeback after another.

Why Can't I Feel Anything?

Even today, four years after the amputation, I don't always know what I am feeling over the loss of my arm. I wish I knew. Sometimes when I watch a video, I will say to myself, "It's no longer there." Literally and figuratively, there is nothing left. Some days I feel as if I'm in a fog, wondering *What am I really feeling about this? What's wrong with you, Dravecky? You lost your arm; you should feel something. Why aren't you connecting with what you feel?*

My inability to feel isn't related to the loss of my arm; there are also other issues of vital importance, but I feel absolutely nothing about them—no register of emotion, just an emptiness. It scares me sometimes.

The thing that scares me most is not being able to feel my relationship to God. There have been times when I don't feel anything for God. Do you know what I mean? Sometimes I feel

God's presence, but other times I do not. That's scary for me, because it can prompt me to start doubting my salvation. So what can I do?

When I lack an emotional connection with God, I have to rely on my faith and God's faithfulness regardless of my feelings. I like the saying I heard somewhere, "Your relationship with God doesn't depend on the puny pebble of your fluctuating faith, but on the massive boulder of his character." I know I have a relationship with God because I am firmly convinced by the truth of the Bible. I know God is real because I can see how he has worked in my life according to his promises. I connect with God intellectually on the basis that he is who he says he is . . . but I want more! I don't want a mere contractual relationship with God. I want a personal, intimate relationship with him that satisfies my head but also touches my heart.

When I was in pain, when it was dark, I didn't want to feel anything, and I considered it an act of God's grace that I could not feel. Knowing the truth without feeling the depth of the pain allowed me to endure.

I think of emotional disconnection like anesthesia. When they amputated my arm, they made sure I could not feel what was going on because it was too painful. Anesthesia is a blessing during surgery—but no one would want to go through all of life under anesthesia.

At some point I went under emotional anesthesia, and I am only now starting to come out of it. Now I *want* to feel because it's not dark anymore; there's a whole lot of light, there are plenty of wonderful things going on, and yet much of the time I am still unable to feel them. I wrestle with this lack of ability to feel a full range of emotions. And I don't think I am alone in this struggle, judging from the reactions of other men.

How did Jan and I and the kids get through it? My wife and I have a strong faith in God. We always believed God was doing something in us through these trials. Even though I didn't always have the strength to seek God, I knew he promised that all things would work together for good (Romans 8:28). I wasn't always clear on what his purpose was for my life, but I trusted he had a purpose. That kept me moving forward.

Of course, there have been times when I have been meeting alone with God and I connected with my emotions. I was able to "feel" him, not just relate to him intellectually. One time I was listening to the "Prayer Song" by Petra, and I found myself crying.

Even though I know that emotion is not everything when it comes to a relationship—whether it's a relationship with God or other people—I am convinced that I'm missing out on something very powerful and important when I can't feel anything. My prayer is that God will help me align my feelings with the truth of his Word, that increasingly he will allow me to experience emotion along with intellectual understanding.

I am still moving forward—two steps ahead, one step back at times—but I am making progress. I am further along today than I was a few years ago. The struggles continue, and there are setbacks, but knowing that life is just one comeback after another helps me to continue the journey.

We've Got to Keep Trying

Relationships are another key area of life that seem to require one comeback after another. Honestly, sometimes they don't seem worth the hassle. When I was talking this issue through while working on the book, I got frustrated even discussing relationships. I believe it is important to have good relationships outside of my family, but sometimes I wish they didn't exist. They can be so difficult.

We all get into situations where we are trying to get along, but one person offends another, hurts his feelings, or blows him out of the water with some unthinking comment. (Stuart Briscoe says, "There's always an evangelical nose out of joint somewhere"; he's right.) And I think, *Forget it! I don't need this hassle. Who gives a flying hoot about developing these relationships? I don't need this.* But then I realize that *I* do. Relationships take work and at times they are frustrating, but every one of us needs meaningful relationships.

I know of many men who were injured by man-to-man relationships, and it was hard for them to be willing to mend the
relationship or even to start a new one. But those who sub-
scribe to the comeback theory have discovered that it's worth
it, despite the pain.

One reason I haven't given up on building relationships is
the connection I discovered between my relationship with God
and the way I relate to people. My relationship with God is vertical while my relationships with others are horizontal, but the
vertical and horizontal lines cross in my heart. If my relationships with people are out of kilter, that usually tells me there is
something off in my relationship with God. If my relationship
with God isn't right, that will mess up how I deal with people.
And that in turn sends my sense of worth as a man plummeting.
This was an incredible revelation to me. If I cannot have the kind
of relationship I want with another person, I usually know why:
It's probably because I lack intimacy with God.

The apostle John saw this connection between the vertical
relationship with God and our horizontal relationships with
each other. He wrote, "Dear friends, since God so loved us, we
also ought to love one another" (1 John 4:11). He went on to say,
"If anyone says, 'I love God,' yet hates his brother, he is a liar. For
anyone who does not love his brother, whom he has seen, cannot love God, whom he has not seen. And he has given us this
command: Whoever loves God must also love his brother" (vv.
20–21). So regardless of whether I feel the need for relationships
or wonder whether they are worth the trouble, the bottom line
is that God says we all need relationships. Loving each other,
even though it is difficult, is where the rubber meets the road.

I am willing to put in the work to have good relationships
because I do not want to go through this life alone and lonely.
Part of the value of the journey of life is time spent with others.
I do not think this journey was meant to be walked alone. We
were made for relationships, and when we are without them, we
cannot possibly feel great about ourselves. None of us can begin

to sense the incredible worth that God has built into us unless we build good relationships.

Hey, I know it isn't easy. I get stuck sometimes. It's hard to say "I'm sorry," or "Please forgive me," or "Maybe I didn't see the whole picture before I blew up." I get stuck—but I am not going to give up. Relationships, like life, are often one comeback after another. We have to stick with it. We cannot just give up because the relationship hits a snag. We must keep trying.

If you attempt a relationship and fail at some point, don't blow it off. Remember, there is more than one out to an inning. It's like I tell my son about baseball: "Just put the ball in play and see what happens. If you don't try, then you will never know." The same thing goes for good relationships. You will never know what good thing might happen if you don't try again.

Where do we start? With the people around us. Start there and see which one of those relationships might become a real friendship. Just keep trying. If you want to have a friend, show yourself to be friendly. You may go through several attempts before you lock into a good relationship, but the key is to keep trying.

There is one last reason I believe we must keep trying to develop good and lasting relationships. Sometimes the only way I can see God is through the eyes of another human being who is willing to stay with me despite the pain. Sometimes we ask, "How does God show his faithfulness to us?" Often all we need to do is look in the eyes of the people around us.

The Bible says, "No one has ever seen God; but if we love one another, God lives in us and his love is made complete in us" (1 John 4:12). I want to get close to God and know his love. He has chosen to deliver that love, primarily, through people. That means that if I cut myself off from relationships with other people, I have cut myself off from receiving God's love. And who wants that? I certainly do not. That is why I am willing to try one comeback after another, especially in relationships. It's the only way.

When God Is Pleased With Our Stumbles

In wrestling with who I am and my worth as a man, I have come to one profound and simple realization: I am a child of God! The worth of a man is found in who he is; and who a Christian man is, is a child of God. And what does it mean to be a child of God? The only way to discover that is to spend time with your heavenly Father.

Jesus said that if we are to enter the kingdom of God, we must become like little children. I think about when my own kids were little, when they were just starting to walk. They would get up, stumble, and fall, and I would help them back up. I enjoyed just watching them.

Now that they are growing up, they can walk just fine, but they still make mistakes; they still fail. Yet I still love them. I want the best for my children, and I will do whatever I can to help them find their way. When they falter, I pick them up and put them back on the right path.

That's precisely how God sees us. We are his little children. How do we relate to God and develop a relationship as his children? The same way kids get to know their father. They've got to be with him. They've got to walk with him. They've got to roast hot dogs with him. They've got to cry over *Charlotte's Web* with him. In a similar vein, that's where we will realize our worth as men, by becoming like little children with our heavenly Father.

C. S. Lewis wrote a great sentence that encourages me in my life's journey: "If we only have the will to walk, God is pleased with our stumbles." Ask anybody who works with me or lives with me, and you'll discover that I stumble plenty. But God knows I have the will to walk. God knows I want to please him, and so I keep taking the next step. If I stumble, I get back up. I am trying to walk in a manner worthy of my Lord and Savior, even though I often hit the pavement.

God knows my heart. I am his child. I rely on his love and his grace. I want to be the man he created me to become. I want to keep my commitments. I want to be of service to others. I want to love God with all my heart, soul, mind, and strength. I want to love others as I love myself.

These desires may seem childishly unrealistic, but I have chosen to walk in this direction. I know I cannot walk this path by my own strength—but I don't have to! I am a child of God, and my Father has taken me by the hand. He tells me I can do all things through Christ who strengthens me (Philippians 4:13), and I believe him.

Life really is just one comeback after another. And every time I stumble, I am determined to make yet another comeback. It's a whole lot better than staying on the floor.

An Eternal Hope

Corrie Ten Boom, whose story is told in *The Hiding Place,* survived Nazi concentration camps to go on to minister the gospel all over the world. Shortly before she went to be with the Lord, friends held a surprise "This is Your Life!" celebration in her honor. Everyone was trying to stay hidden so Corrie would not suspect anything, but she happened to run into Joni Earickson Tada sitting in her wheelchair in a hallway. Joni is a quadraplegic who has ministered hope and encouragement to millions.

Corrie was frail by this time, her shoulders bent from age and the abuse she endured at the hands of the Nazis. She took Joni's hands in her wrinkled ones, leaned close to her, and whispered with her thick Dutch accent, "One day, Joni, you and I will dance together in heaven."[1]

These two women have found the strength to live, the strength to suffer, and even the strength to face death with hope. Jesus Christ has given them the power within to cope with the decaying conditions of their bodies and the varying circumstances of life.[2] One found that power in a Nazi death camp; the other found it sitting in a wheelchair.

They knew that the secret to living in hope, even though we may be broken in this life, is to know the promise of the resurrection. Jesus died a real death. He endured real pain. He was laid in a real tomb. He was raised in a real body to prove that death had really been conquered. He gave us real hope to believe that, just as he was raised from the dead, we too will be raised. We will be changed and our mortal bodies will put on immortality.

Like Corrie and Joni, we too will dance together in heaven. And what a glorious comeback that will be!

Notes

1. Story told by Bruce Barbour.

2. Cf. Jürgen Moltmann, *The Power of the Powerless* (San Franscisco: Harper & Row), p. 142, as quoted in Philip Yancey, *Where is God When It Hurts* (Grand Rapids: Zondervan, 1990), p. 186.

Chapter Fifteen

When the End Comes

What would you do if a doctor said you had only six to eight weeks to live? It's hard to imagine, isn't it? But Jim Andrews didn't have to imagine it; that was exactly his prognosis.

I met Jim last summer, two weeks after his doctor gave him the grim news. Jim and his wife, Leslie, came to our office for support and encouragement. Jan and I invited them to our home for dinner. After dinner, Jim and I sat and talked about life and death and what is really important. He had ceased to bargain with God. Jim was only forty years old, but he had accepted the fact that, barring a miracle, the inoperable tumor growing in his brain would take his life in a matter of weeks.

You learn a lot from a man who knows his life here on earth will wrap up in less than two months. Talking with Jim made me realize that we start out in life aiming to achieve something in our career—have a family, accumulate wealth, whatever—but when the doctor gives you the news that your time is up, those things are not what matter most. It's love that matters, taking care of your family, communicating all the things you want your kids to learn from you, making sure your wife knows how much you appreciate her, and ensuring that your family has good memories of your times together. That is certainly what mattered most to Jim Andrews.

Jim worked as an independent real estate appraiser. He worked diligently over the years to provide for his family and give quality service to his clients. The day the doctor told him he had only weeks left to live, he closed up shop. His clients missed him, but they all understood. He was a good man who did a good job, but his work on earth was done—at least in that office.

Jim spent his last weeks getting everything in order so that his wife would be able to go on without him as best she could. He put their financial affairs in order. His diligence and wise business dealings allowed him to leave her financially set, so she didn't have to go to work. He wrote a letter to twenty-four Christian men with whom he had built relationships over the years, in which he asked them to be a support to his wife and three young sons, since he would not be around to protect them. You have already read about the letter he wrote to his sons, affirming their worth in his eyes, expressing his love, and trying to communicate his values and wisdom to help them make the most of their lives. He started a love letter to his wife, but he was never able to finish it. Still, Leslie knew how dearly he loved her.

At the funeral, people came from far and wide to honor Jim. He wasn't rich or famous, but he was an inspiration to many people. A man recently told Leslie that whenever he has an important decision to make, he stops to ask himself, "What would Jim Andrews do in this situation?" Jim lived a good life, loved God, loved his family, and—from our earthly perspective— died too soon.

I did not know Jim very long, but he taught me something of great importance about the worth of a man. He taught me how our God-given worth can be effectively lived out in this life. He taught me how a man who understands his own worth can in turn make all those around him see and feel their own worth. He taught me that the worth of a man is not merely some abstract theological idea, but has huge practical implications that spill over into every area of life.

This man accepted God's will for him, even though he could not understand why God would take him away from his family. He did not go out kicking and screaming about how unfair it was that he should die so young. He went out expressing love to others, making his passing as easy as possible for them. He lived and died with love for God and for others. Love is the greatest expression of the worth of a man; Jim Andrews taught me that.

Jim was grateful that he could spend his last days focused on preparing his family for his passing instead of having to rush around trying to patch up unresolved hurts and mending broken relationships. Jim didn't feel the weight of guilt or regret. He could focus on loving his family and friends to the end.

If you were Jim, how would you spend your final days on earth? Maybe thinking about what you would need to do if you only had two months to live would help you figure out what is really worthwhile in your life for the long haul. I know that is what happened with me.

When People Look Back on My Life

For three weeks in 1995, I thought I might be dying. I began to have severe stomach pains and feared the cancer was back. An MRI eventually showed I was fine, although the doctor suspected that stress had given me a peptic ulcer. It's amazing what fear of imminent death can do to transform a man. During those three weeks, I came running every time my son or daughter called out to ask for something. It's remarkable how much our relationship grew in those three short weeks. They would say, "Dad, come tuck us in," and I would go running upstairs and tuck them in to bed, sit there patiently, and give them a big hug.

Now that I no longer face the threat of impending death, I must admit that I am not as attentive as I was then. Yet that experience showed me how little it takes to love my kids more fully.

At the end of my life, whenever that time comes, I want my kids to say, "He was a great dad." I want my wife to say, "He was a great husband!" If people say only, "He was a great baseball player," I would be devastated. I hope people will say, "Dave Dravecky was a Christian who happened to be a baseball player," not "a baseball player who happened to be a Christian." I have come to realize that the people I love and the God I serve mean a lot more than baseball ever will, even though the game meant a great deal to me. I agree with Paul Azinger, the pro golfer, who said, "It's great to be a PGA member, believe me. And great to be a PGA winner. But the greatest thing of all in life is to be called a child of God."[1]

An acquaintance said to me once, "I went to a funeral the other day, and these people all stood up and started talking about the guy who had died. It turned my stomach, because everything I was hearing was a lie. My friend and I were sitting together at the funeral trying to be respectful as they talked about this guy being a great teacher, when in fact he was a lousy teacher. My friend and I weren't the only ones obviously embarrassed by the things these people made up. You know, Dave, when I die, I don't want people to have to lie about me. I want them to be able to tell the truth."

That's a powerful goal to motivate a man's life, isn't it? When people look back on my life, I don't want them to have to lie about me.

Facing death has a powerful effect on how you live life. How many people facing death say, "I wish I had spent more time at work"? Yet how many say, "I wish I had given more time and love to my family"? As I faced the real threat of death when cancer invaded my body, I lived more true to the man I want to be. The threat of death reminded me that I have only one chance here on earth.

Now that the threat of cancer has been cut away, I ask God to remind me that I can be sure only of today. There are no guarantees for any of us as to when our time will come. When I keep my focus on how brief and fragile life is, I live life more true to my highest aims and more true to those I love. By thinking about what I want people to remember when they look back on my life,

I see more clearly what I must do today to make sure I go out a winner. I especially want my kids to appreciate the heritage I am leaving them—and I am leaving them one, good or bad. And so are you.

Jonathan's Blessing

On "Father's Blessing Day" at Jonathan's school, the father of each student was asked to come to class and give a blessing to his child. Each man was expected to prepare a letter that he would read aloud. We were supposed to take turns reading our blessing to our son or daughter in front of all the other kids and dads. When I arrived, everyone seemed apprehensive. A tentative feeling in the room told me I wasn't the only one thinking, *I'm not too sure about this. How's this going to come off?*

The first guy read his letter, and it was the most beautiful letter I have ever heard. I thought, *Holy smokes, I didn't write that kind of letter*. We went around in a circle, and each father did a wonderful job. With each one, I was wishing I had spent more time preparing my blessing for Jonathan.

This event was very important to Jonathan. He looked forward to me being available for this one day. He kept asking me, "You're not speaking on this day, are you? You're not out of town? Make sure you're gonna be there." And I told him, "Nope, I don't have any other plans. I'm gonna be there." So as I sat there waiting for my turn, I was praying that I wouldn't let him down.

Talk about a challenge! Try doing an biography on your kid when he's only ten years old. What do you talk about? That he's a great home-run hitter? A kid hasn't had time to rack up a bunch of accomplishments, so I decided to talk about my son in terms of who he is and what we love about him.

Finally it was my turn. I started off by saying, "Jonathan, I still remember when you were born. We were in San Diego, and your mom and I thought you were going to be a girl. When you were only halfway out, the doctor pulled you up and made you look at mom. He waved your hand and said, 'Hi Mommy!' Then Jonathan, you just torpedoed out; I mean, you came out with such force the doctor almost dropped you. You know what, buddy? You've kept right on going that way—like a torpedo every day since." Jonathan got a chuckle out of that.

Next I focused on his nature, some of the special things he does that bring joy to us. I talked about his sense of humor, about how we bust up laughing every time he does a Jim Carey imitation. I said, "You bring so much joy into our home because of your laughter." I talked about his sensitivity toward kids, especially little kids, and his compassion toward others. Then I threw in, "We're still working on your compassion and sensitivity toward your sister."

He was sitting there with his eyes fixed on me as I described all these wonderful traits of his and how I felt about him. Then I said, "You know, Jonathan, I hope you always trust God with all your heart and don't lean on your own understanding, but acknowledge God in all your ways so he will make your paths straight. You're my best friend and I love you, Bud!" That was it.

All of a sudden, my son broke down in tears. He threw his arms around me and just sobbed on my shoulder for a full five minutes. He was the first child to have an emotional reaction. He just wept and wept. I wasn't sure whether I had embarrassed him. He continued to sob as the next letter was read and the next. I bent over and whispered in his ear, "Are you okay? Did I make you upset?"

"No," he said.

"Jonathan, did I embarrass you?" I asked.

"No."

"Are you crying because of what I said?"

"Yes, but it's okay. I liked what you said," he told me between sobs.

I could barely contain the sense of wonder and love I felt at that moment. That was one of the most precious moments in my life, because I realized how powerful my love and approval is to my son. It was just so sweet.

Our kids need to hear how much they mean to us. We need to take the time to clarify our thoughts about what is special about each child. Writing that letter helped me appreciate the qualities in Jonathan that I sometimes take for granted. Giving that blessing changed my focus. It turned my attention away from the negative things that are difficult to deal with and reminded me of the positive qualities that I treasure in my child. When Jonathan reacted as intensely as he did, that told me something that is too often forgotten: Our love and approval is worth the world to our kids.

I think a big part of what we are supposed to do here on earth is to learn to love each other. As I said earlier, love is the greatest expression of the worth God has built into us. I don't always love as I should, but I'm learning. And that is the necessary first step.

What Is Your Game Plan?

When I was pitching, I used to go over my game plan with the catcher. We would get together before the game and look at the lineup, and he would ask, "How do you want to pitch to these guys?" That gave us a sense of where we were headed. After being with a catcher for a while, we didn't have to do that so much, because we got to know each other and both of us knew what the game plan would be, based on shared principles. If the catcher knew my game plan, he could help me stay on course. He might call a time-out and say, "Now, Dave, according to your game plan, you don't want to be doing this. So why are you heading in this direction?"

I found that helpful in baseball, and I find it helpful in life. That is why I am part of a group of men who are committed to holding each other accountable to stay true to our game plans. General principles in keeping with the basic tenets of the Bible guide my decision making. I want to be faithful to God, my family, my friends, and my calling. I want to live with integrity and make the most of my talents and the opportunities I am afforded in life. I want to love God with all my heart, soul, mind, and strength, and to love my neighbor as myself. Those are the general principles that shape my game plan. The guys in my accountability group share those basic values.

Beyond general beliefs and values, it helps to make specific commitments. The guys in my accountability group share specific commitments regarding our schedules, our activities, and even our areas of temptation (as much as we dare). In a sense, we look over the lineup of what we are facing and tell each other how we hope to deal with it successfully.

For example, I intend to cut back on my speaking schedule during the coming year so I can focus on spending enough time with my family and leading the Outreach of Hope ministry. It isn't easy for me to decline requests, and I have a tendency to say yes to invitations without thinking about how it will impact the other important areas of my life. I have talked this over with the guys in my accountability group and let them know my specific game plan. A few weeks back, I asked Bob Knepper, a member of my group, to take me to the airport. There was a lot going on at the ministry, and I was distracted and troubled by having to fly off to speak when I believed I was needed at the office. He could see I was struggling and asked, "Are you sure you are doing what God has called you to do? I heard you say you want to wear the hat of leadership for the ministry, but it seems hard for you to keep switching hats between speaking and leading the ministry." He didn't tell me what he thought I should do; he just called a time-out to remind me of the game plan I had gone over with him earlier.

May I suggest that you take some time to clarify your own game plan for life? You can call it your game plan, mission statement, list of promises, principles to live by, or whatever—just make sure you know what you are aiming for. Then sit down with a friend or a small group of guys who share your values, go over the game plan with them, and give each other permission to call time-out whenever any of you start to stray from it. It will not only keep you out of trouble, it will also encourage you more than I can possibly describe. And it will be a huge encouragement to your loved ones, especially when it comes time for you to check out of this life.

When Death Comes Knocking

Not long ago I received a request to visit a hospitalized friend who was in the final stages of terminal cancer. This man was in his mid-forties, an extremely successful businessman, and a single parent of two elementary school-age children. His wife had died the previous year after a horse-riding accident. Financially, my friend and his children were set for life—but not for death.

Even though we deal with cases like this every day in our ministry, they are never routine. I approached that hospital room with the kind of awesome respect that comes over me whenever I am invited to the side of the dying. If I ever have a sense of walking on sacred ground, it's when I stand near a deathbed. I entered that room with great respect for this man and his situation. I was concerned for him and was willing to talk about issues of eternal importance, but I had no intention of forcing the issue.

I don't know what I expected. A lot depends on the family and the kinds of relationships a person has built during his life. When I entered the room, several other people were milling about. A TV was on in the upper corner of the room, tuned to a football game. I was praying silently that I would have the opportunity to talk with my friend about his final destination.

After exchanging introductions and nervous smiles, the other people who had been visiting excused themselves. My friend's eyes were fixed on the football game. "Hey, how about those 49ers?"

"Great play, huh?"

"Yeah, great play." Then the room went silent.

In a few moments my eyes met his and this dear man began to weep. "What is going to become of my children?" he sobbed. He looked back at the game for a moment, then he said to me, "Dave, I know you have something to tell me. Please do."

I had prayed for this moment before I ever came up to the room. I had asked the Lord, "Just allow him to see Jesus in me." But now I felt so awkward. I was supposed to be the encourager, but I was scared to death. Understand, this man was a genius. I felt pretty feeble as the deliverer of a message that could mean eternal life or death—but I was the one with the opportunity, so I took my best shot.

Struggling to overcome my nerves, I anxiously tried to get the right words out. As best I could I tried to explain my hope of heaven. I told my friend that Jesus Christ had died on the cross to pay for my sins as well as for his. I explained that I wanted him to have that same hope, to know that after he died he would be with Jesus. In the few moments I had, I did my best—but when I was done, I was sure I had blown it.

Soon the group of visitors returned and my friend's eyes moved back to the football game on the TV screen. I said my good-byes and left, positive that I would not be seeing him again. I left there feeling totally inadequate. This guy was a mental giant and I felt as if I had stumbled all over a Sunday school lesson written for first graders. I consoled myself that at least he knew I cared about him. I prayed for him and trusted the rest to God.

Ten days later a mutual friend, a Christian, called to tell me our friend had died. He also told me about a conversation they had about a week after my visit. He wanted to make sure that his dying friend understood the gospel, so he said to him, "I have something to share with you. Are you willing to listen?" When our friend said he was, this mature believer carefully explained the Christian message and told his friend that he could be sure of a home in heaven if he would pray to accept Christ into his life. "Will you pray for me?" the dying man asked.

"No, I won't," his friend gently replied. "This is a decision you have to make for yourself. You must pray on your own behalf. Would you like to?"

The man very much wanted to, and when he was through, the angels held a party in heaven to celebrate another addition to God's family. My friend who led this man to the Lord had called to say that I had played a part in our friend's decision for Christ. I had planted the seed; my friend had watered it; and God brought new growth. I was overjoyed to hear the report.

You know, when you are on your deathbed, things that once were complicated become quite simple. That man prayed to commit his spirit into the care of God through the grace and forgiveness of Jesus Christ. It did not take impressive words to convince him that in the final evaluation it wasn't his money, or his position, or who was winning the football game that mattered. Those things didn't matter at all. All that mattered was the sure hope of heaven.

In this book we have talked about the worth of a man from many different perspectives, but I dare not end this chapter without reminding you of one of the most important questions Jesus posed about the worth of a man: "What will it profit a man, if he gains the whole world, and forfeits his life [or soul]?" (Matthew 16:26, RSV).

When you come to the inevitable, which is death, good principles or good business success or even genius aren't enough to get you into heaven. You can get by in this life with a positive attitude and not have the Lord, but if you die without receiving the salvation that comes only by trusting Jesus Christ, you have no hope. You're history.

Once a person crosses the divide between life and death, it's a whole different ball game. It is so easy to get distracted from the eternal things of life, but it is so important to make sure that it doesn't happen. When it comes to the end, all of us must answer the one question that no one can avoid: Where will I go when I die? I firmly believe that without Jesus as your Savior, you go to hell; with him, you go to heaven. It is that simple, and it is that important. When it comes to the worth of a man, it's the ultimate decision.

The End of the Road

Much thought and prayer has gone into the creation of this book. After writing *Comeback* and *When You Can't Come Back*, Jan and I knew another book was needed to bring the story to completion. A few years back, when I began trying to decide what this book should be and what to call it, I kept gravitating toward the idea of my life as a journey. For a while I thought this book would be titled, *Uncharted Journey*. Eventually we set that idea aside because I wasn't ready to write another book at that time, but the concept of my life as a journey stayed with me. That's the term that best helps me understand what God has brought me through.

I used to think I could map out my life and get wherever I wanted to go. I tried to chart my course in a way that would please God, but I always had a predetermined destination in mind. Never in my wildest dreams did I imagine that my life would end up where it is today. *This* destination wasn't even on my map.

Cancer took me way off course, but I worked hard to return to where I wanted to be. The best I could do at that juncture was to keep putting one foot in front of the other, keep praying, and cooperate with the doctors. Once I made my comeback to baseball, I thought that was the part of the story where the rainbow appeared over the horizon and we could call in a happy ending. But we all know that is not what happened.

Something far more profound took place, something bigger than baseball. God decided to take me off-road to find lasting hope. That hope was not to be found in a career, a ballpark, or a seven-figure salary. That hope was a person, Jesus Christ, who would go with me wherever the journey took me.

When God took me down another road, one that wasn't on my map, he taught me that Dave Dravecky the man has something to offer, something more valuable than Dave Dravecky the baseball player or Dave Dravecky the comeback kid. What I have to offer is a message of hope to every man on the journey of life. I offer hope—hope that doesn't disappoint even when life does, hope for the journey even when the road seems to plummet into the valley and wind through the wilderness.

The Legacy We Leave Behind

I really like the television series *Touched by an Angel*. In each episode, the angels, Tess and Monica, are assigned to bring God's message of love and hope to the characters in the story and help them find their way through life's experiences. The angels appear first in human form, but usually at some point reveal themselves as God's messengers. Each character must then choose how to respond to God's message.

One of my favorite episodes revolves around a baseball coach who showed real promise as a player early in life, but who never made it to the big leagues because of a war injury. He never quite gets over his loss, and although he can occasionally forget his troubles while hanging out with his friends, the bitter taste of his lost dream sours him on life. He takes out his frustrations on the young baseball players he coaches at his old high school.

As the story unfolds the coach discovers he has terminal cancer. But rather than take advantage of the little time he has left, he becomes even more surly and focuses his rage on a young player who just may have the talent to make it to the major leagues. The coach doesn't think the player is giving 100 percent, and it infuriates him, especially since the young man looks up to the coach as the father he never had.

As the tension builds and clashes between player and coach grow more frequent, the angels try to help the coach understand that he has the power to give this young player a phenomenal gift—the gift of his support, not just the benefit of his experience. But he refuses to listen.

As the coach's time on earth grows shorter, he seems no closer to a change of heart than he was at the beginning; if anything, he appears even more angry and distant. The only thing he seems to care about is an old baseball bat he has carried with him ever since his playing days. It is his prized possession and he allows no one near it—especially his talented younger player, whom he thinks is wasting his gifts. By the show's end it looks as if the coach is going to check out of this life without ever giving his player the encouragement he longs for.

But in a dramatic eleventh hour twist, the angels finally get through to the coach. At last he understands what an incredible gift he has in his power either to give or to withhold from his star player. In a moving climax, the coach solemnly hands his prized bat to the young man. In that instant we know that more than a stick of wood has been offered; the coach has given his blessing to the young man, along with encouragement to go out on the ball field (and in life) and become all he can be.

While it is unlikely that two angels named Monica and Tess will appear at the end of our lives to help us leave this world on a high note, we can allow Hollywood's creation to remind us that we are all leaving behind a legacy. It is within our power either to bless our loved ones with the encouragement to become all they can be, or to withhold that blessing. One day it will be our turn to check out of this life and into the next. Most of us won't have a prized baseball bat to hand over, but all of us can give the priceless blessing that only we have the power to offer.

In coming to understand more of my worth as a man, I have also come to understand the incredible worth of those around me. A big part of the legacy I want to leave behind is the certainty in people's minds that I love them and that God has built into them more worth than any of us will ever fully realize. That is the gift the coach in the story finally gave his young friend, and that is the gift I want to present to my own loved ones.

When it is my time to go, I want my family and friends to know how much they are "worth" to me. I want them to know my love. I want them to feel and experience the enormous worth that God has built into them as his creations and children. But one thing I do not want: I do not want to wait until I lay gasping on my deathbed to tell them.

The Full Worth of a Man

Guys, each of us is on a journey, an uncertain journey called life. God never said it was going to be easy, but it can surely be worthwhile. God will walk this journey with us. Wherever our road leads us, he will go with us and will be there at the end of the road, waiting for us with open arms and with love in his eyes.

That's what the worth of a man is all about. That's where true worth comes from. And to know God's infinite love is to know the full worth of a man.

Notes

1. Watson Spoelstra, "Waddy's World," *Sports Spectrum Magazine*, June, 1995.

Epilogue:
What's a Dave Dravecky Worth These Days?

When I arrived in Sacramento to work on this book, Pat and Connie Neal picked me up at the airport. We swung through Arby's and stopped by their house so I could eat before going to my hotel. Taylor, their red-headed six-year-old son, came barreling down the stairs and into the kitchen.

"Hi, are you Dave Drabecky?" (He has a hard time with the 'v' sound.)

"Yeah, I sure am." I offered him my hand and he reached out to shake it enthusiastically. He was a friendly kid, not a bit shy. He kept on talking while I ate my ham and cheese.

"Hey, Dave, my mom read me the book about you. Can you show me your secret moves so I can grow up to be a famous baseball player like you?"

I had a mouth full, so I couldn't answer him. He just kept on talking.

"If I grow up to be a famous baseball player, I could get a million dollars. My friend Johnny said I could, so could you show me your secret moves?"

Obviously this was important to him. You could see the excitement in his eyes. I looked at my left side, trying to figure out for a moment if there was some way I could help the kid out. "Taylor, I can't show you my secret moves, because I used to pitch with my left arm and I don't have a left arm anymore."

"Oh, yeah—I saw that in the book."

"But if you want to be a baseball player when you grow up, the most important thing is to practice." Once he saw there were no secret moves to be had, he seemed to lose interest in baseball. My missing arm now became the focus of his curiosity.

"Can I see it?" he asked as he shot me an inquisitive look.

"Sure." I put my sandwich down and pulled up the sleeve of my T-shirt to give him a look.

"Can I touch it?" His younger sister watched tentatively as I nodded, and Taylor began rubbing his hands over the stump of what used to be my once-famous pitching arm. "Oooh! Cool!"

With that, Taylor and I became buddies. I gave him an autographed photo of me pitching for the Giants. A couple of days later his mom told me about a conversation they had as she tucked him into bed. He was really excited about having my autographed picture because one of the boys told him it was worth a thousand dollars. He wanted to know whom he could sell it to so he could collect his loot. She explained to him that it wasn't worth a thousand dollars.

"Then what's it worth?" he asked.

"Well, its worth isn't measured in money. It's supposed to remind you of Dave."

"Oh. . . . ." He thought for a moment, then said, "Well, that's okay, too. I like Dave."

"Dave Drabecky, ONE ARM!"

That Sunday morning I went to church with the Neals. I gave a short greeting to the congregation at the request of the pastor, so people came up after church to meet me. Taylor was waiting around, watching all these folks huddled around me and asking for my autograph. It took a while to politely greet everyone who wanted to meet me, so the kids played around while waiting. Eventually we made our way toward the van, saying good-bye as we went. It was quite an accomplishment when we finally got everyone into the vehicle. The kids were in the back, Pat took his place behind the wheel, and I sat in the front passenger seat. My door was still open, since I was talking to the pastor and his wife.

Just then a door opened from the church and the children's pastor emerged. Taylor whipped off his seatbelt and yelled, "Open the door! Open the door! I've got to tell pastor Cori something."

He seemed so eager that Connie agreed to open the side door of the van. Taylor popped his head out and yelled across the driveway, "Hey, Pastor Cori—look!" He pointed proudly to me and shouted, "Dave Drabecky, ONE ARM!" He said it as if he had made some great discovery, as if she hadn't noticed. We all cracked up.

In his own six-year-old way, Taylor was trying hard to figure out who I was, what I was worth, and what made me special to so many people—exactly what I had been trying to figure out myself. Finally he summed up my identity in two words: ONE ARM. No doubt those words describe what I lost in life. But is that truly what determines who I am?

In his brief encounters with me, this little boy summed up the ways I have tried to find my worth as a man. During progressive seasons of life, I looked for my identity and worth in dreams of becoming a major league baseball player, in hopes of fame and fortune, and in the cheers of the crowd. When I lost my arm, I had to reevaluate my worth as a man. I asked myself, "If I found my worth by reaching my dreams, did I lose it when I could no longer perform the 'secret moves' that brought me fame and fortune? Had I become a has-been, defined only by what I had lost?"

After a long struggle, I finally know for sure the answer to that question. The answer is NO. While I always "believed" that my worth and identity were found in Jesus Christ alone, it wasn't until I struggled through the emotional turmoil caused by the loss of my arm that I came to *know* I was worth more than what I had accomplished, more than what I had gained or lost. I am a man created in the image of God, in the process of being recreated in the image of Christ. That gives me unimaginable worth, regardless of what I can or cannot do.

When Taylor introduced me as, "Dave Drabecky, ONE ARM!" I first thought that the arm he mentioned was the one I lost. He probably meant the arm I have left; that's all he can see. It's my choice as to which one I focus on. Do I focus on what I have lost and what I am no longer able to do? Or do I focus on who I am and what I have to offer? That is really a choice every man has to make, regardless of what form his losses might take.

A Man Is Greater Than His Works

Jan and I have a friend, Carla Muir, who writes poetry. She can write a poem about almost anything, but what I like about Carla's work is how she captures the heart of the matter. When I started work on this book, I asked Carla to write a poem about the worth of a man. Her poem captures something important I have learned.

A Man's True Worth

I once believed that what I did
placed value on my worth.
And walking where great men have walked,
I saw my dream give birth.

But dreams don't always last through life;
in fact, they often die.
The day I watched my dream pass on—
all alone stood I.

And in the searching of my soul,
God gave to me new peace.
Today I'm living other dreams—
the kind that will not cease.

In Jesus' eyes I'm valued so
much greater than I see.
My worth is not in what I do;
it's in Christ's death for me.

—Carla Muir

What I used to do was important both to me and to many of my fans; but at last I have learned that my worth is not summed up in what I did. My worth was not lost when I could no longer pitch, nor did it increase when I began a new career track.

Today I realize that the worth of other men is not found in what they can do either. No, their worth is found in whom God has made them to be. Period. They are made in his image and have been redeemed by his life—and those things do not change, regardless of how circumstances might.

Reflecting the Character of God

Before my arm was amputated I was hospitalized with a staph infection. My agent, Sealy Yates, flew to New York to be with me. He did not come to work out a deal. He did not come to advise me. He came as a brother in Christ who cared about me as a friend.

Sealy is a highly respected attorney who also works as a literary agent in Christian publishing. It was great that he was a good attorney, that he had a good reputation in the Christian community, and that he was able to provide incredible service to us by negotiating book deals and representing us. But none of those work-related things were as important as the time he invested in me.

Sealy is a great example of why I say that it is not what we do that gives us worth, regardless of how valuable our work may be. When Sealy slept on that cot in my hospital room, he did something far more valuable than representing me as a legal advisor or literary agent. I appreciate his work, but his worth far exceeds his works. He reflects to me something of the very character of God. The image of Christ is stamped across his very soul.

Now, if I can accept that Sealy the man is worth far more than his works, I must also accept that my worth is not found in the work I do, but in what God has done in and for me.

My wife would tell you that this discovery is continuing to shape and mold my attitudes and actions perhaps more than any other single force. I am more at peace with myself and others than I have ever been. I would be the first to admit that I still ocassionally struggle with my worth as a man, and I continue to miss not having a left arm, but these struggles are growing fewer and less turbulent. I expect the struggle in some form will continue for the rest of my life—but the major difference today is that I know how it's going to turn out.

Let me leave you with some favorite words from the apostle Paul, who knew a thing or two about a man's worth. The apostle knew that a man's understanding of his worth affected not only his life, but everyone whom he touched:

> Now the Lord is the Spirit, and where the Spirit of the Lord is, there is freedom. And we, who with unveiled faces all reflect the Lord's glory, are being transformed into his likeness with ever-increasing glory, which comes from the Lord, who is the Spirit.

> Therefore we do not lose heart. Though outwardly we are wasting away, yet inwardly we are being renewed day by day. For our light and momentary troubles are achieving for us an eternal glory that far outweighs them all. So we fix our eyes not on what is seen, but on what is unseen. For what is seen is temporary, but what is unseen is eternal.
>
> (2 Corinthians 3:17–18; 4:16–18)

For further information on Dave Dravecky's Outreach of Hope ministry or for information regarding speaking engagements, please contact:

Dave Dravecky's Outreach of Hope
13840 Gleneagle Drive
Colorado Springs, CO 80921
719-481-3528
www.outreachofhope.org

Do Not Lose Heart
Meditations of Encouragement and Comfort
Dave and Jan Dravecky
with Steve Halliday

Illustrated by Thomas Kinkade

"Therefore we do not lose heart. Though outwardly we are wasting away, yet inwardly we are being renewed day by day. For our light and momentary troubles are achieving for us an eternal glory that far outweighs them all. So we fix our eyes not on what is seen, but what is unseen. For what is seen is temporary, but what is unseen is eternal."
–2 Cor. 4:16-18

Sooner or later suffering touches us all. It may be personal pain—the loss of a mate, a debilitating illness, a financial disaster. It may be the pain of someone we're close to—a friend or loved one whose grief leaves us groping for words of comfort.

Dave and Jan Dravecky understand suffering, having gone through the fires of cancer and depression themselves. Based on the Scripture passage that has become the Draveckys' motto, 2 Corinthians 4:16-18, this book of meditations is for people who are struggling. People who need a few wise, uplifting words from fellow Christians who know what it's like to hurt—Dave, Jan, and other well-known Christian writers have contributed to this book to bring together exactly the comforting words that hurting people need to hear.

Featuring the luminous artwork of nationally renowned painter Thomas Kinkade, *Do Not Lose Heart* is a comforting and uplifting union of word and image.

Softcover 0-310-24043-3

ZONDERVAN™

GRAND RAPIDS, MICHIGAN 49530 USA

WWW.ZONDERVAN.COM

Stand by Me
A Guidebook of Practical Ways to Encourage a Hurting Friend

Dave and Jan Dravecky with Amanda Sorenson

"I want to help, but I don't know how." If you've ever been close to someone who's hurting, you know the feeling. What do you say? What *don't* you say?

This small, practical book offers guidance for helping and encouraging a friend or loved one in a time of pain. It's also for the hurting ones, framing their experiences in words they can relate to. Drawn from a variety of sources, each short perspective showcases a different way to stand by the hurting, on each page pairing one brief, insightful gem of writing with an inspirational quote or verse of Scripture. This jewel-like book makes a wise companion for people who care—and for those who, in the midst of their pain, will appreciate the quick doses of comfort this book is full of.

Softcover 0-310-21646-X

ZONDERVAN™

GRAND RAPIDS, MICHIGAN 49530 USA

WWW.ZONDERVAN.COM

Called Up

Stories of Life and Faith from the Great Game of Baseball

Dave Dravecky with Mike Yorkey

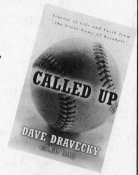

During eight seasons of major league baseball, pitcher Dave Dravecky learned more than the importance of getting ahead in the count or wasting a pitch when he had the batter in the hole with an 0-2 count. Baseball taught him lessons he could apply to his life and his relationship with God. That's what *Called Up* is about.

In this fast-moving and compelling book, Dravecky retells classic baseball stories and introduces readers to some of baseball's greatest players—and characters. You'll actually feel the tension as you relive the final three outs in Sandy Koufax's electrifying no-hitter against the Chicago Cubs in 1965. Taking you inside the game, his insights will prompt you to think and be encouraged about your own performance in the game of life.

God doesn't waste any pitches when it comes to teaching you about life from the game of baseball. You'll love the breezy stories, the timeless thoughts, and the funny quotes in *Called Up*.

Hardcover: 0-310-25230-X

ZONDERVAN™

GRAND RAPIDS, MICHIGAN 49530 USA

WWW.ZONDERVAN.COM

Dravecky:
A Story
of Courage and Grace
Available on video!

Here is the Dravecky story on video. It's more than
just a baseball film—it's the story of a family's
struggle to overcome incredible obstacles through
tenacity and faith. It provides a unique avenue to
creatively and compellingly share the Gospel.
Viewers will experience the clear and
uncompromising testimony of Dave and Jan
Dravecky as they share how their reliance on Christ
enabled them to meet life's challenges.

0-310-24599-0

ZONDERVAN™

GRAND RAPIDS, MICHIGAN 49530 USA

WWW.ZONDERVAN.COM

We want to hear from you. Please send your comments about this book
to us in care of zreview@zondervan.com. Thank you.

GRAND RAPIDS, MICHIGAN 49530 USA

WWW.ZONDERVAN.COM